I0015144

MACHINE LEARNING

A Complete Guide for Beginners to Mastering the
Fundamentals of ML. Learn about Machine Learning,
Artificial Intelligence, Deep Learning and their Application
in Finance and Business

By

Mike Cowley

Respective authors own all copyrights not held by the publisher.

The information herein is offered for informational purposes solely, and is universal as so. The presentation of the information is without contract or any type of guarantee assurance.

The trademarks that are used are without any consent, and the publication of the trademark is without permission or backing by the trademark owner. All trademarks and brands within this book are for clarifying purposes only and are the owned by the owners themselves, not affiliated with this document.

TABLE OF CONTENTS

INTRODUCTION --8

A BRIEF HISTORY ---11

CHAPTER ONE--13

WHAT IS MACHINE LEARNING---13

TYPES OF MACHINE LEARNING --15

HOW DOES MACHINE LEARNING WORK? -------------------------------------20

THE DISTINCTION AMONG ARTIFICIAL INTELLIGENCE AND MACHINE LEARNING
--25

CHAPTER TWO--28

DEEP LEARNING --28

TEN TYPES OF USES OF DEEP LEARNING ----------------------------------29

THE MACHINE LEARNING TOOLBOX: ADVANCED ALGORITHMS-----------------38

A CAREER IN THE FIELD OF MACHINE LEARNING IS NOT AN EASY TASK: REQUIRES
A LOT OF EFFORT AND TIME---40

CHAPTER THREE --43

APPLICATION OF MACHINE LEARNING-----------------------------------**43**

MACHINE LEARNING IN FINANCE ---**51**

WHY CONSIDER MACHINE LEARNING IN FINANCE? ---------------------------------52

PROCEDURE AUTOMATION---53

MACHINE LEARNING IN BUSINESS--**63**

POINTERS FOR APPLYING MACHINE LEARNING TO BUSINESS PROBLEMS-----------68

CHAPTER FOUR --**74**

THE IMPACTS OF MACHINE LEARNING-----------------------------------**74**

MACHINE LEARNING ISN'T JUST FOR ADVANCED FIRST ORGANIZATIONS -------**78**

KEY CONSIDERATIONS AND IMPLICATIONS-----------------------------------**83**

SPOTLIGHT: INDUSTRY IMPLICATIONS -----------------------------------**85**

CHAPTER FIVE --**89**

THE MOST POWERFUL MACHINE LEARNING TECHNIQUES IN DATA MINING --**89**

THE DIFFERENCE BETWEEN DATA MINING AND MACHINE LEARNING---------**100**

POTENTIAL USES FOR A REAL-TIME SYSTEM -------------------------------106

CRITICAL PATTERNS OF MACHINE LEARNING-------------------------------108

CHAPTER SIX ---**116**

UTILIZING AI AND DECISION TREE FOR SENTIMENT ANALYSIS ---**116**

THE BASICS OF DECISION TREES ---**127**
DISTINCTIVE ALGORITHM TYPES --131

CHAPTER SEVEN ---**135**

CHALLENGES OF MACHINE LEARNING -------------------------------------**135**

ORGANIZING THE MACHINE LEARNING PROCESS AND CHALLENGES -----------**140**
THE THREAT OF ADVANCED AI--**144**

CONCLUSION ---**151**

INTRODUCTION

Machine Language or ML empowers computers to learn and act without being unequivocally modified. It advances from the investigation of example acknowledgment and the structure and examination of calculations to empower gaining from information and settle on potential information-driven expectations or choices. It is so inescapable today that a significant number of us likely use it a few times each day without knowing it.

In prior phases of investigation advancement, the organizations that most profited from the new field were the data firms and online organizations that saw and took advantage of the lucky breaks of huge information before others. The capacity to give genuinely necessary information and data spoke to an unmistakable first mover's bit of leeway for these organizations. While the first movers in quite a while were the huge victors, their favorable position won't last any longer as efficiency levels out. The development to Analytics 3.0 is a distinct advantage because of the scope of business issues that savvy mechanization — a blend of AI — can unravel its expansion each day. At this stage, each firm in any industry can benefit from clever computerization. Organizations that invest promptly in AI can increase long haul benefits, benefitting from crafted by examination pioneers. To pick up these advantages, organizations must revaluate how the investigation of information can make an incentive for them with regards to Analytics 3.0.

Enormous changes are hatching in the showcasing scene, and these movements are, to a great extent, down to the power ML. Such is its effect that 97% of pioneers accept the eventual fate of promoting will comprise of keen advertisers working in a joint effort with AI-based mechanization elements.

ML methods are utilized to tackle a large group of different issues, and organizations continue to profit a lot as we veer towards a universe of hyper-joined information, channels, substance, and setting. For the advanced advertising group, ML is tied in with discovering bits of prescient information in the influxes of organized and unstructured data and utilizing them to further your potential benefit.

The capacity to react rapidly and precisely to changes in client conduct is basic in this day and age, and AI. In this article, we investigate the ML advancements that are being utilized successfully, and its potential uses crosswise over organizations. AI is firmly identified with human-made brainpower. It very well may be viewed as order inside it. The historical backdrop of AI can enable us to comprehend it better so let us experience a fast outline.

A BRIEF HISTORY

As is regularly the situation with new advancements, it is difficult to pinpoint precisely when in time the introduction of ML occurred. Frequently, individuals who go the extent of doling out a date to its commencement are extremely simply disclosing to you the date some basic idea was presented.

Here we receive an increasingly reasonable view:

1950 to 1980: We have the beginning times of AI. From the production of the Turing Test (A test to advise whether a machine's capacity to show keen conduct is proportional to, or vague from, that of a human.) to the making of the main neural system structure for computers and fundamental applications, for example, improving computers' presentation in the round of checkers and unpleasant example acknowledgment.

1980 to 2000: We see instances of computers making a general guideline from info (preparing information), the way to express words in a beginning time and the specialization of projects spoken to by the notorious chess coordinate among DeepBlue and Garry Kasparov finishing in a thrashing as the then best on the planet.

2000 to 2010: Geoffrey Hinton coins the expression "Deep conviction organizes," the model term for Deep learning calculations, which take the information and cause progressive changes on them until we have the yield. ImageNet, a broad visual database, is made for visual item acknowledgment.

2010 to 2019: We hear more about vast information, information science Deep learning, and fake neural systems increasingly. In 2010, Deep learning developed as the following stage in AI strategies. In 2016, Google's AlphaGo (a Deep learning-based programming) beats the world's best players of GO, a game considered ordinarily harder than chess.

CHAPTER ONE
WHAT IS MACHINE LEARNING

Before we adventure off on our voyage to ad-lib what is presumably the greatest field of study, research, and improvement, it is just able and fitting that we comprehend it first, regardless of whether at a fundamental level. AI, otherwise called Analytics 3.0, is the most recent improvement in the field of information examination. ML enables PCs to take in a lot of information, process it, and show themselves new abilities utilizing that input. It's a method to accomplish Artificial Intelligence, or AI, using a "learn by doing" process.

In this way, to give a concise outline to comprehension, ML for short is one of the most blazing and the most inclining advances on the planet right now, which is gotten from and fills in as a backup use of the field of Artificial Intelligence. It includes utilizing plenteous bits of discrete datasets to make the incredible frameworks and PCs of today modern enough to comprehend and act how people do. The dataset that we provide for it as the preparation model chips away at different basic calculations to make PCs significantly wiser than they as of now are and help them to get things done humanly: by gaining from past practices.

Necessities of Making Great Machine Learning Frameworks

So what is required for making such insightful frameworks? The following are the things required in making such machine learning frameworks:

- Information - Input information is required for foreseeing the yield.

- Calculations - Machine Learning is reliant on certain factual calculations to decide information designs.

- Computerization - It is the capacity to cause frameworks to work consequently.

- Cycle - The total procedure is iterative for example, redundancy of the procedure.

- Versatility - The limit of the machine can be expanded or diminished in size and scale.

- Displaying - The interest makes the models by the way toward demonstrating.

TYPES OF MACHINE LEARNING

ML comes in a wide range of varieties, contingent upon the calculation and its destinations. You can gap AI calculations into fundamental gatherings dependent on their motivation:

+ Supervised learning

+ Unsupervised learning

+ Reinforcement learning

+ Batch learning

+ Online learning

+ Instance-based learning

+ Model-based learning

Supervised learning

Supervised learning happens when an algorithm gains from model data and related objective reactions that can comprise of numeric qualities or string marks, for example, classes or labels, to later anticipate the right response when presented with new models. The

15

directed methodology is without a doubt, like human learning under the supervision of an educator. The educator gives genuine guides to the understudy to retain, and the understudy at that point gets general principles from these particular models.

You have to recognize relapse issues, whose target is a numeric worth, and arrangement issues, whose target is a subjective variable, for example, a class or a tag. A relapse assignment decides the reasonable costs of houses in the Boston territory, and a characterization errand recognizes sorts of iris blooms dependent on their sepal and petal measures.

Unsupervised Learning

Unsupervised learning happens when a calculation gains from plain models with no related reaction, leaving for the calculation to decide the information designs without anyone else. This kind of calculation will in general, rebuild the information into something different, for example, new includes that may speak to a class or another arrangement of uncorrelated qualities. They are very helpful in giving people bits of knowledge into the importance of information and new valuable contributions to administered machine learning calculations.

As a sort of learning, it takes after the strategies people use to make sense of that specific articles or occasions are from a similar class, for example, by watching the level of likeness between items. Some suggestion frameworks that you find on the web through advertising computerization depend on this sort of learning.

The showcasing robotization calculation gets its recommendations from what you've purchased previously. The proposals depend on an estimation of what gathering of clients you take after the most and afterward surmising your conceivable inclinations dependent on that gathering.

Reinforcement learning

Reinforcement learning happens when you present the calculation with models that need names, as in unsupervised learning. Be that as it may, you can go with a model with positive or negative input by the arrangement the calculation proposes. Support learning is associated with applications for which the calculation must decide (so the item is prescriptive, not only spellbinding, as in unsupervised learning), and the choices bear results. In the human world, it is much the same as learning by experimentation.

Mistakes help you learn because they have a punishment included (cost, loss of time, lament, torment, etc.), instructing you that a specific game-plan is less inclined to prevail over others. An intriguing case of support learning happens when PCs figure out how to play computer games independent from anyone else.

For this situation, an application gives the calculation instances of explicit circumstances, for example, having the gamer stuck in a labyrinth while evading an adversary. The application tells the calculation of the result of moves it makes, and learning happens while attempting to maintain a strategic distance from what it finds to be hazardous and to seek after survival. You can view how the organization Google DeepMind has made a fortification learning program that plays old Atari's videogames. When viewing the video, see how the program is at first awkward and untalented yet consistently improves with preparing until it turns into a victor.

Batch Learning

In this sort of ML frameworks, the framework can't adapt steadily: the framework must get all the required information. That implies it will require numerous assets and an immense measure of time, so it's constantly done disconnected. Along these lines, to work with this sort of learning, the main activity is to prepare the framework, and after that, dispatch it with no learning.

Web-based Learning

This sort of learning is something contrary to batch learning. I imply that, here, the framework can adapt gradually by giving the framework all the accessible information as occasions (gatherings or exclusively), and afterward, the framework can learn on the fly. You can utilize this sort of framework for issues that require the nonstop progression of information, which additionally needs to adjust rapidly to any changes. Likewise, you can utilize this kind of framework to work with enormous informational indexes. You should know how quick your framework can adjust to any adjustments in the information's "learning rate." If the speed is high, it implies that the framework will adapt rapidly, yet it likewise will overlook old information rapidly.

Instance-based learning

This is the least difficult kind of discovering that you ought to learn by heart. By utilizing this learning in our email program, it will signal the majority of the messages that were hailed by clients.

Model-based learning

There is another taking in where gaining from models enables development to make forecasts.

HOW DOES MACHINE LEARNING WORK?

ML utilizes forms like that of information mining. The calculations are portrayed regarding objective function(f) that maps the input variable (x) to a yield variable (y). This can be spoken to as:

$$y=f(x)$$

There is additionally a blunder e, which is autonomous of the information variable x. In this manner the more summed up type of the condition is:

$y=f(x) + e$

The normal sort of AI is to gain proficiency with the mapping of x to y for forecasts. This technique is known as prescient displaying to make the most exact expectations. There are different suppositions for this capacity.

Awful and Insufficient Quantity of Training Data

ML frameworks dislike youngsters, who can recognize apples and oranges in a wide range of hues and shapes. However, they require part of the information to work adequately, regardless of whether you're working with straightforward projects and issues, or complex applications like picture handling and discourse acknowledgment. Here is a case of the preposterous viability of information, demonstrating the MS venture, which incorporates straightforward information and the unpredictable issue of NLP.

Low-Quality Data

In case you're working with preparing information that is brimming with blunders and exceptions, this will make it exceptionally difficult for the framework to identify designs so that it won't work appropriately. Thus, on the off chance that you need your program to function admirably, you should invest more energy tidying up your preparation information.

Insignificant Features

The framework might have the option to learn if the preparation information contains enough highlights and information that aren't excessively superfluous. The most significant piece of any ML undertaking is to grow great highlights "of highlight building."

Highlight Engineering

The procedure of highlight designing goes this way:

+ Choice of highlights: choosing the most helpful highlights.

Extraction of highlights: joining existing highlights to give increasingly helpful highlights.

+ Production of new includes: formation of new includes, in light of information.

Testing

In the event that you'd like to ensure that your model is functioning admirably and that model can sum up with new cases, you can evaluate new cases with it by placing the model in nature and afterward checking how it will perform. This is a decent strategy, yet if your model is deficient, the client will gripe.

You should partition your information into two sets, one set for preparing and the second one for testing, with the goal that you can prepare your model utilizing the first and test it utilizing the second. The speculation blunder is the pace of mistake by assessment of your model on the test set. The worth you get will let you know whether your model is sufficient, and on the off chance that it will work appropriately.

If the blunder rate is low, the model is great and will perform appropriately. Interestingly, if your rate is high, this implies your model will perform seriously and not work appropriately. My recommendation to you is to utilize 80% of the information for preparing and 20% for testing purposes, with the goal that it's extremely easy to test or assess a model.

Overfitting the Data

In case you're in an outside nation and somebody takes something of yours, you may state that everybody is a criminal. This is an overgeneralization, and, in AI, is classified "overfitting." This implies machines do something very similar: they can perform well when they're working with the preparation information. However, they can't sum them up appropriately. For instance, in the accompanying figure, you'll locate a high level of life fulfillment model that overfits the information. However, it functions admirably with the preparation information.

When does this happen?

Overfitting happens when the model is perplexing for the measure of preparing information given.

Solutions

To tackle the overfitting issue, you ought to do the accompanying:

- Gather more information for "preparing information."

- Reduce the commotion level

- Select one with fewer parameters

Underfitting the Data

From its name, underfitting is something contrary to overfitting, and you'll experience this when the model is exceptionally easy to learn. For instance, utilizing the case of personal satisfaction, genuine is more mind-boggling than your model so that the expectations won't yield the equivalent, even in the preparation models.

Solutions

To fix this issue:

- Select the most dominant model, which has numerous parameters.

- Feed the best includes into your calculation. Here, I'm alluding to highlight the building.

- Reduce the imperatives of your model.

THE DISTINCTION AMONG ARTIFICIAL INTELLIGENCE AND MACHINE LEARNING

Artificial intelligence is the idea of machines performing assignments that are normal for human knowledge — it is the comprehensive stage that is featured in different Sci-Fi motion pictures like Terminator, Matrix, and so on. The idea of AI is to address things like perceiving items and sounds, getting the hang of, arranging, and critical thinking.

Today the greater part of the AI utilized in a business setting is explicit to one territory; it shows attributes of the human knowledge in one explicit zone like sound, picture acknowledgment or critical thinking. The advancement of AI to duplicate various parts of human insight is the following stage in its development, and that is the focal point of new rising AI activities crosswise over businesses.

ML, in its most fundamental structure, is an approach to accomplish AI. AI is a method for preparing a calculation with the goal that it can figure out how to learn. The preparation here includes encouraging a lot of information into a calculation and enabling the calculation to change itself and improve. To further develop this, AI can be accomplished without AI by composing noteworthy measures of code or projects. However, today, AI calculations make the way toward making AI-based applications a lot simpler than through manual procedures.

Basic Misguided Judgments About Artificial Intelligence and Machine Learning

Individuals regularly believe that Artificial Intelligence (through AI) will supplant their activity capacities totally and perform at a higher level than people, or that AI has human-level feelings and knowledge. Normally, these come from a misconception concerning what AI can do. While it is equipped for handling a lot of information rapidly, it's not at human-level as far as judgment and discernment. There's likewise a misguided judgment (regularly powered by science fiction motion pictures) that AI applications will all of a sudden become conscious. Artificial intelligence could wind up dangerous, however not at the level regularly depicted in Hollywood. A last misguided judgment is that AI is a silver shot. Simulated intelligence can tackle a lot of things, yet there's not one enchantment calculation that can understand everything. Most AI applications should be fabricated and actualized for a particular reason, dependent on the business and friends.

CHAPTER TWO
DEEP LEARNING

Deep Learning is a piece of the more extensive field of machine learning and depends on information portrayal learning. It depends on the translation of an artificial neural system. Deep Learning calculation utilizes numerous layers of processing. Each layer utilizes the yield of a past layer as a contribution to itself. The calculation utilized can be administered calculation or unsupervised algorithms.

There are many uses for Deep learning — everything from the voice-initiated highlights of your advanced colleague to self-driving vehicles. Utilizing deep learning to improve your everyday life is decent. However, the vast majority need different motivations to grasp innovation, for example, finding a new line of work. Luckily, Deep learning doesn't simply influence your capacity to find data quicker yet additionally offers some truly fascinating openings for work, and with the "goodness" factor that solitary Deep learning can give. This section gives you a review of ten fascinating occupations that depend on Deep learning somewhat today. This section speaks to help distinguish a few occupations that utilize deep learning rapidly, and more are included each day.

TEN TYPES OF USES OF DEEP LEARNING

Deep learning can help when overseeing individuals

A frightening motion picture called The Circle would have you accept that cutting edge innovation will be much more intrusive than Big Brother in the book 1984, by George Orwell. Some portion of the film's story includes introducing cameras all over — even in rooms. The fundamental character gets up each morning to welcome everybody who is watching her. Truly, it can give you the creeps if you let it.

Be that as it may, genuine deep learning isn't tied in with checking and making a decision about individuals, generally. It's increasingly similar to Oracle's Global Human Resources Cloud. A long way from being terrifying, this specific innovation can make you look savvy and over every one of the exercises of your day. The video is a little absurd, however, it gives you a smart thought of how deep learning can at present make your activity simpler.

Deep learning improves prescription

Deep learning is influencing the act of prescription from multiple points of view, as it should be obvious when you go to the specialist or invest energy at an emergency clinic. Deep learning helps with diagnosing diseases and discovering their right fix. Deep learning is even used to improve the indicative procedure for difficult to-recognize issues, including those of the eye. In any case, one of the most significant uses for Deep learning in the medicine field is research.

The basic demonstration of finding the right patients to use for research designs isn't generally that basic. The patients must meet severe criteria, or any testing outcomes may demonstrate invalid. Specialists currently depend on deep learning to perform errands like finding the correct patient, structuring the preliminary criteria, and advancing the outcomes. Drug will require many individuals who are prepared both in prescription and in the utilization of deep learning systems for medication to keep accomplishing progresses at their present pace.

Deep learning grows new gadgets

Advancement in certain regions of computer innovation, for example, the fundamental framework, which is currently a product, has backed off throughout the years. Be that as it may, development in regions that as of late ended up suitable has enormously expanded. A creator today has more potential outlets for new gadgets than any other time in recent memory. One of these new territories is the way to perform deep learning assignments. To make the potential for performing deep learning undertakings of more prominent multifaceted nature, numerous associations presently utilize specific equipment that surpasses the capacities of GPUs — the as of now favored preparing innovation for deep learning.

Deep learning can give client assistance

Numerous Deep learning dialogs allude to chatbots and different types of client care, including interpretation administrations. On the off chance that you're interested, you can have an intelligent involvement with a chatbot at Pandorabots.com. The utilization of chatbots and other client care advancements have worked up concern, nevertheless.

Some shopper bunches that state human client care is damned, as in this Forbes article. Regardless, if you ever needed to manage a chatbot to perform anything complex, you realize the experience is not exactly engaging. So the new worldview is the human and chatbot mix.

Deep learning can enable you to see information in new ways

Take a gander at a progression of sites and other information sources, and you see a certain something: every single present datum in an unexpected way. A computer doesn't comprehend contrasts in introduction and isn't influenced by some look. It doesn't get information; it searches for examples. Deep learning is empowering applications to gather more information all alone by guaranteeing that the application can see proper examples, notwithstanding when those examples contrast from what the application has seen previously. Even though deep learning will improve and accelerate information gathering, notwithstanding, a human will, in any case, need to translate the information. People still need to guarantee that the application gathers great information because the application genuinely sees nothing about information.

Another approach to see information in new ways is to perform information expansion. Once more, the application does the snort work, yet it takes a human to figure out what kind of expansion to give. As it were, the human does the imaginative, intriguing part, and the application walks along, guaranteeing that things work.

Deep learning can perform investigation quicker

At the point when the vast majority talk about investigation, they consider an analyst, some researcher, or a master. In any case, deep learning is getting to be dug in some intriguing spots that will require human cooperation to see full use, for example, anticipating car crashes.

Envision a police division allotting assets dependent on traffic stream designs with the goal that an official is as of now holding up at the site of a typical mishap. The police lieutenant would need to realize how to exploit the utilization of this sort. This specific use hasn't occurred at this point. However, it likely could because it's as of now plausible utilizing real innovation. So performing examination will never again be a vocation for those with "Dr." before their names; it will be for everybody.

Examination, without anyone else's input, isn't too valuable. It's the demonstration of consolidating the examination with a particular need in a specific domain that winds up valuable. What you do with investigation characterizes the impact of that examination on you and everyone around you. A human can comprehend the idea of investigation with a reason; a deep learning arrangement can play out the examination and give a yield.

Deep learning can help create a superior workplace

Deep learning will improve your life and your work progressively, agreeable on the off chance that you happen to have aptitudes that enable you to interface effectively with ML. This section portrays how ML could change the work environment later on. A significant component of this dialog is to make work all the more welcoming.

At a certain point in humankind's history, work was charming for many people. It isn't so much that they went around singing and snickering constantly; it's that numerous individuals looked forward to beginning every day. Afterward, during the mechanical transformation, other individuals put the strongest workers into work, making each day from work the main joy that a few people appreciated. The issue has turned out to be extreme to such an extent that you can discover well-known melodies about it, such as "Working for the Weekend." By expelling the menial worker from the work environment, deep learning can make work agreeable once more.

Something that you don't see referenced regularly is the impact on efficiency of a falling birth rate in created nations. This McKinsey article takes this issue somewhat and gives a diagram demonstrating the potential effect of Deep learning on different ventures. If the present pattern keeps, having less accessible laborers will mean a requirement for enlargement in the work environment.

In any case, you may think about your future, whether you stress that you probably won't have the option to adjust to the new reality. The issue is that you may not realize whether you're sheltered. You can much find how you may wind up functioning in space sooner or later. Lamentably, not every person needs to make that kind of move, much as the Luddites didn't during the modern insurgency. Eventually, society will turn out to be essentially unique about what it is today because of AI — much as the mechanical upheaval has officially changed society.

Deep learning can help research dark or point by point data

Computers can do a certain thing — design coordinating — outstandingly well (and much superior to people. On the off chance that you've at any point had the inclination that you're skimming in data, and none of it identifies with your present need, you're not the only one. Data over-burden has been an issue for a long time and compounds each year. You can discover a ton of counsel on managing data over-burden. The issue is that regardless, you're suffocating in data. Deep learning empowers you to discovers the needle in a sheaf and in a sensible measure of time. Rather than months, a great deep learning arrangement could discover the data you need in only hours by and large.

Notwithstanding, realizing that the data exists is normally not adequate. You need data that is nitty-gritty enough to completely address your inquiry, which frequently means finding more than one source and combining the data. Once more, a deep learning arrangement could discover examples and squash the information together for you with the goal that you don't need to consolidate the contribution from numerous sources physically.

Deep learning can help plan structures

The vast majority see engineering as an innovative exchange. Envision planning the following Empire State Building or some other structure that will stand the trial of time. Before, planning such a structure took years. Strangely, the contractual worker constructed the Empire State Building in only barely a year, yet this isn't generally the situation. Deep learning and computers innovation can help decrease an opportunity to structure and fabricate structures extensively by permitting things like virtual walkthroughs. The utilization of deep learning is improving the lives of planners in critical ways.

Be that as it may, transforming a structure into a virtual visit isn't even the most noteworthy accomplishment of deep learning in this field. Utilizing deep learning empowers architects to find potential building issues, perform pressure testing, and guarantee security in different ways before the plan ever leaves the planning phase. These capacities limit the number of issues that happen after a structure winds up operational, and the designer can appreciate the trees of a triumph as opposed to the contempt and potential disaster of a disappointment.

Deep learning can improve security

Mishaps occur! Be that as it may, deep taking in can help keep mishaps from occurring — in any event generally. By dissecting complex examples continuously, deep learning can help individuals who are engaged with different parts of wellbeing affirmation. For instance, by following different traffic designs and foreseeing the potential for a mishap well ahead of time, a deep learning arrangement could furnish security specialists with proposals for keeping the mishap from occurring by any stretch of the imagination. A human couldn't play out the investigation as a result of an excessive number of factors. Nonetheless, a deep learning arrangement can play out the examination and afterward give yield to a human to potential execution.

Deep Neural Network

Deep Neural Network is a sort of Artificial Neural Network with numerous layers that are covered up between the information layer and the yield layer. This idea is known as a highlight chain of importance, and it will result in general, an increment of the multifaceted nature and reflection of information. This enables the system to deal with extremely enormous, high-dimensional informational collections having a large number of parameters. The Neural Network can also be applied in the area listed above.

THE MACHINE LEARNING TOOLBOX: ADVANCED ALGORITHMS

The fundamental motivation behind ML is to create algorithms that can "learn" from the information. Algorithms are consecutive forms that can take care of an issue in a limited number of steps. In ML algorithms, each bit of information that is gone through the calculation pipeline will impact the result of the calculation. For instance, if one spam message is gone through the calculation, the machine will realize what one spam message resembles. If a huge number of spam messages are gone through the calculation, the machine has been presented to a huge number of spam messages with the goal that it can recognize shared traits and better characterize precisely what spam resembles. The objective of ML is to build up an algorithm that can autonomously work and be applied to novel information. In this model, it would be an algorithm that can precisely arrange an email as "spam" or "genuine."

In supervised learning, precisely described information is separated into "preparing" and "test" sets. Preparing sets are normally about 80% of the information, and test sets are the rest of. In our model, we have messages that are delegated "spam" or "real" by human specialists. The ML algorithms are created utilizing the preparation set, a bit of a message that has just been recognized. When the upgraded algorithm has been created after the majority of the preparation set has gone through the pipeline, the algorithm is tried with the test set to decide its exactness. Precision is dictated by how often the algorithm accurately portrays test set information. In a perfect world, calculations would arrange enormous information effectively 100% of the time. Yet, thinking about that, there are consistent anomalies that aren't reasonable. An order precision above 90% is generally viewed as worthy.

In unsupervised learning, the classes are not known. The ML algorithm would deduce examples and properties dependent on information correlations and bunch information into various gatherings. For the email model, after running a huge number of unclassified messages through the algorithm, the algorithm may gather them into three distinct classifications. Human specialists would then look indiscriminately at tests from the three groups of messages, and upon assessment, may mark them as "spam," "individual," and "retail." Or on the other hand, maybe four groups of messages would be produced by the calculation. All things considered, human specialists would dissect models in each group and allocate bunch marks, for example, "spam," "individual," "work," and "retail." Note that unsupervised learning yield requires master investigation to dole out importance.

A CAREER IN THE FIELD OF MACHINE LEARNING IS NOT AN EASY TASK: REQUIRES A LOT OF EFFORT AND TIME

The career requires a great deal of self-learning. The angles to be remembered as a learner is per the following:

a) The hypothetical perspectives related to Arithmetic, Statistic, Computer Science, Operations Research, other ML hypotheses are required to be seen appropriately to increase a top to bottom information about them.

b) 'Learning by doing' is a well-known saying which expresses that the hypothetical viewpoints can be seen adequately and Deeply if these ideas are applied essentially. Programming in dialects, for example, R, Python, and so forth; working with the databases; managing the huge information, philosophies, and strategies; encountering information wrangling and envisioning the discoveries as reports and so forth.

It is important to note that landing the positions in this field requires a ton of experience. The significant work experience can be picked up by working in lesser situations in the organizations doing a great deal of expository work. Encountering examination would give you a chance to move from an information examiner to an information researcher or ML.

Work experience scarcely matters in the new companies since they require the people who try for self-learning capacity.

The work environments where you are locked in an attempt to discover the undertakings including ML. It isn't important to take a shot at the activities related to your activity profile; you can stay at work longer than required by taking a shot at certain tasks that are not identified within your activity profile yet goes consummately with your ranges of abilities. It would let you have a decent impression over your chief, which would further prompt advancements. It may prompt an adjustment in your job in the association. This would lead you to the guide of your vocation in this field.

Along these lines, work experience can be picked up by making you qualified for the rumored employments of the top fortune organizations in this field.

The activity profiles related to AI incorporates Software Engineer, Software Developer, and Data Scientist, and so on. The normal pay bundle of an AI designer adds up to $1,000,000 per annum. The compensation bundle fluctuates with the measure of work experience you gain and the aptitudes sets you procure step by step.

Continuously attempt to learn to an ever-increasing extent. The new knowledge would give you a chance to investigate the new zones in your working environment. Learn constantly.

CHAPTER THREE
APPLICATION OF MACHINE LEARNING

The mystical bit of baffling science makes our life more agreeable and best than previously. In our regular day to day existence, the commitment of science is simply evident. We can't neglect or overlook the impact of science in our life. Since, at present, we are habituated to the Internet in numerous means of our everyday life, i.e., to experience an obscure course now we utilize a Google map, to express our musings or sentiments utilize informal communities, or to share our insight use sites, to know the news we utilize online news entrances, etc. If we attempt to comprehend the impact of science in our life, at that point, we will see that really; these are the result of utilizing AI and ML applications. As of late, there has been a sensational flood of enthusiasm for the period of ML, and more individuals become mindful of the extent of new applications empowered by the ML approach. It fabricates a guide to make contact with the gadget and make the gadget reasonable to react to our directions and directions. In this section, we attempt to catch the mind-blowing ongoing utilization of ML, which will make our view of life progressively computerized. Be that as it may, some of the best utilization of ML is recorded here.

1. Picture Recognition

Picture recognition is one of the hugest ML and human-made consciousness models. Fundamentally, it is a methodology for recognizing and distinguishing an element or an article in the computerized picture. Besides, this procedure can be utilized for further investigation, for example, design acknowledgment, face location, face acknowledgment, optical character acknowledgment, and some more.

Even though few systems are accessible, using an AI approach for picture acknowledgment is ideal. In an AI approach for a picture, acknowledgment is included extricating the key highlights from the picture and accordingly input these highlights to an AI model.

2. Notion Analysis

Notion examination is another continuous ML application. It additionally alludes to supposition mining, notion arrangement, and so forth. It's a procedure of deciding the demeanor or assessment of the speaker or the author. As it were, it's the way toward discovering the feeling from the content.

The primary worry of feeling investigation is, "what other individuals think?". Expect that somebody composes 'the film is slightly below average.' To discover the real idea or feeling from the content (is it positive or negative) is the undertaking of supposition investigation. This assessment examination application can likewise apply to the further application, for example, in audit-based site, basic leadership application.

The MI approach is a control that builds a framework by separating the information from information. Also, this methodology can utilize huge information to build up a framework. In the AI approach, there are two kinds of learning calculations managed and unaided. Both of these can be utilized to supposition investigation.

3. News Classification

News grouping is another benchmark use of an AI approach. Why or How? Now that the volume of data has developed enormously on the web, each individual has his individual intrigue or decision. Along these lines, to pick or accumulate a bit of proper data turns into a test to the clients from the sea of this web.

Giving that fascinating classification of news to the objective readers will, without a doubt, increment the worthiness of news locales. Besides, readers or clients can scan for explicit news successfully and proficiently.

There are a few strategies for ML for this reason, i.e., bolster vector machine, gullible Bayes, k-closest neighbor, and so forth. Additionally, there are a few "news arrangement programming" is accessible.

4. Video Surveillance

A little video record contains more data contrasted with content reports and other media documents, for example, sound, pictures. Consequently, removing valuable data from video, i.e., the mechanized video reconnaissance framework, has turned into a hot research issue. With this respect, video reconnaissance is one of the propelled use of an ML approach.

The nearness of a human in an alternate casing of a video is a typical situation. In the security-based application, the ID of the human from the recordings is a significant issue. The face example is the most broadly utilized parameter to perceive an individual.

A framework with the capacity to assemble data about the nearness of a similar individual in an alternate casing of a video is exceptionally requesting. There are a few techniques for MLalgorithm to follow the development of humans and recognizing them.

5. Speech Recognition

Speech acknowledgment is the way toward changing expressed words into the content. It is moreover called programmed discourse acknowledgment, computer speech acknowledgment, or discourse to content. This field is profited by the progression of the ML approach and enormous information.

46

At present, all business reason discourse acknowledgment framework utilizes an ML way to deal with perceive the speech. Why? The speech acknowledgment framework utilizing the ML approach beats superior to the discourse acknowledgment framework utilizing a customary technique.

Since, in an ML approach, the framework is prepared before it goes for approval. Fundamentally, the ML programming of discourse acknowledgment works at two learning stages: 1. Before the product buy (train the product in a free speaker space) 2. After the client buys the product (train the product in a subordinate speaker area).

This application can likewise be utilized for further investigation, i.e., human services area, instructive, and military.

6. Online Fraud Detection

Online extortion identification is a propelled utilization of the ML algorithm. This methodology is down to earth to give cybersecurity to the clients productively. As of late, PayPal is utilizing an ML and computerized reasoning calculation for tax evasion. This propelled ML, and computerized reasoning model lessens the misfortune and amplifies the benefit. Utilizing ML in this application, the discovery framework ends up stronger than some other customary principle-based framework.

7. Characterization

Characterization or arrangement is the way toward ordering the articles or cases into multiple predefined classes. The utilization of the ML approach makes a classifier framework progressively unique. The objective of the ML approach is to manufacture a brief model. This methodology is to improve the effectiveness of a classifier framework.

Each case in an informational collection utilized by the ML and AI is spoken to utilizing a similar arrangement of highlights. These cases may have a known mark; this is known as the directed ML algorithm. Conversely, on the off chance that the names are known, at that point, it's called the unsupervised. These two varieties of the ML methodologies are utilized for arrangement issues.

8. Regression

Regression is another utilization of ML. There are a few procedures for regression that are accessible.

Assume, X1, X2, X3 ,... .Xn is the info factor, and Y is the yield. During this case, utilizing AI innovation to give the yield (y) on the possibility of the info factors (x). A model is utilized to exact the association between various parameters as beneath:

Y=g(x)

Utilizing the ML approach in regression, the parameters can be enhanced.

9. Suggestion for Products and Services

Assume that; we bought a few things from an online shop a few days prior. Within two or three days, you will see that the related shopping sites or administrations are prescribed for you.

Once more, you search something in google in this way after your looking. The comparative sort of things is prescribed for you. This suggestion of items and administrations are the development use of AI strategy.

A few ML strategies like managed, semi-directed, solo, support are utilized to build up these items proposal based framework. This sort of framework likewise worked with the consolidation of enormous information and ML method.

10. Language Identification

Language distinguishing proof (Language Guessing) is the way toward recognizing the sort of language. Apache Open NLP, Apache Tika, is the language distinguishing programming. There are a few ways to deal with distinguish the language. Among these, the AI and human-made consciousness approach are productive.

MACHINE LEARNING IN FINANCE

ML in finance may do something amazing, even though there is no enchantment behind it (well, perhaps only a tad). In any case, the accomplishment of ML undertaking depends more on structure proficient foundation, gathering appropriate datasets, and applying the correct calculations.

ML is making noteworthy advances in the finance-related administration's industry. We should perceive any reason why budgetary organizations should mind, what arrangements they can actualize with ML and AI, and how precisely they can apply this innovation. Most finance-related administrations organizations are as yet not prepared to remove the genuine incentive from this innovation for the accompanying reasons:

- Businesses regularly have unreasonable desires towards ML and its incentive for their associations.
- R&D in ML is expensive.
- The lack of DS/ML specialists is another significant concern. The figure underneath represents a touchy development of interest for ML and AI aptitudes.
- Financial occupants are not deft enough with regards to refreshing information foundation.

Despite the difficulties, numerous budgetary organizations, as of now, exploit this innovation. They do it for a lot of valid justifications:

- Reduced operational costs because of procedure computerization.

- Increased incomes because of better profitability and upgraded client encounters.

- Better consistency and fortified security.

There is a wide scope of open-source ML algorithms and apparatuses that fit extraordinarily with budgetary information. Also, settled budgetary administration organizations have significant subsidies that they can stand to spend on cutting edge registering equipment. Because of the quantitative idea of the money related space and enormous volumes of recorded information, ML is ready to improve numerous parts of the budgetary environment. That is the reason such a significant number of money related organizations are investing vigorously in AI R&D. Concerning the slowpokes, it can demonstrate to be expensive to disregard AI and ML.

PROCEDURE AUTOMATION

Procedure computerization is one of the most widely recognized utilization of ML in finance. The innovation permits to supplant manual work, computerize redundant errands, and increment profitability.

Subsequently, ML empowers organizations to advance expenses, improve client encounters, and scale-up administrations. Here are robotization use instances of ML in account:

- Chatbots
- Call-focus computerization.
- Paperwork computerization.
- Gamification of representative preparing, and that's just the beginning.

The following are a few instances of procedure computerization in banking:

JPMorgan Chase propelled a Contract Intelligence (COiN) stage that use Natural Language Processing, one of the ML methods. The arrangement forms authoritative reports and concentrates basic information from them. Manual audit of 12,000 yearly business credit understandings would ordinarily take up around 360,000 work hours.

Though, ML permits to audit a similar number of agreements in only a couple of hours.

BNY Mello incorporated procedure mechanization into their biological financial system. This advancement is in charge of $300,000 in yearly investment funds and has realized a wide scope of operational enhancements.

Wells Fargo utilizes an ML-driven chatbot through the Facebook Messenger stage to speak with clients and give help passwords and records.

Privatbank is a Ukrainian bank that executed chatbot collaborators over its versatile and web stages. Chatbots accelerated the goals of general client inquiries and permitted them to diminish the number of human associates.

Security

Security dangers in the fund are expanding alongside the developing number of exchange, clients, and outsider mixes. Also, ML algorithms are astounding at identifying fakes.

For example, banks can utilize this innovation to screen a great many exchange parameters for each record continuously. The calculation analyses each move a cardholder makes and surveys if an endeavored action is normal for that specific client — such model spots fake conduct with high accuracy.

When the framework recognizes suspicious record conduct, it can demand extra distinguishing proof from the client to approve the exchange. Or on the other hand, even obstruct the exchange through and through, if there is in any event 95% likelihood of it being a fake. ML algorithms need only a couple of moments (or even split seconds) to survey an exchange. The speed forestalls fakes continuously, not simply spot them after the wrongdoing has just been submitted.

Money related observing is another security use case for ML in a fund. Information researchers can prepare the framework to identify countless micropayments and banner such tax evasion systems as smurfing.

ML algorithms can altogether improve organize security, as well. Information researchers train a framework to spot and disconnect digital dangers, as ML is best in class in breaking down a large number of parameters and constant. What's more, odds are this innovation self-discipline the most developed cybersecurity organizes in the nearest future.

Adyen, Payoneer, PayPal, Stripe, and Skrill are some outstanding fin-tech organizations that invest intensely in security ML.

Guaranteeing and credit scoring

ML algorithms fit superbly with the guaranteeing errands that are so normal in account and protection.

Information researchers train models on a large number of client profiles with several information passages for every client. A well-prepared framework would then be able to play out the equivalent endorsing and credit-scoring errands in genuine situations. Such scoring motors help human representatives work a lot quicker and all the more precisely.

Banks and insurance agencies have an enormous number of chronicled customer information, so they can utilize these sections to prepare ML models. On the other hand, they can use datasets created by enormous telecom or service organizations.

For example, BBVA Bancomer is working together with an elective credit-scoring stage Destacame. The bank plans to build acknowledge access for clients for a meagre record as a consumer in Latin America. Destacame gets to charge installment data from service organizations using open APIs. Utilizing charge installment conduct, Destacame produces a FICO assessment for a client and sends the outcome to the bank.

Algorithmic exchanging

In algorithmic exchanging, ML settles on better-exchanging choices. A numerical model screens the news and exchange results constant and recognizes designs that can power stock costs to go up or down. It would then be able to act proactively to sell, hold, or purchase stocks as indicated by its expectations.

ML calculations can break down a large number of information sources at the same time, something that human brokers can't in any way, shape, or form accomplish.

ML algorithms help human merchants crush a thin advantage over the market normal. Furthermore, given the huge volumes of exchanging tasks, that little advantage frequently converts into critical benefits.

Robo-warning

Robo-consultants are currently typical in the monetary space. As of now, there are two noteworthy uses of ML in the warning area.

Portfolio, the board, is an online riches the executives' administration that utilizations calculations and insights to assign, oversee and streamline customers' advantages. Clients enter their present monetary resources and objectives, state, sparing a million dollars by the age of 50. A robo-counselor at that point assigns the present resources crosswise over venture openings dependent on the hazard inclinations and the ideal objectives.

A suggestion of monetary items. Numerous online protection administrations use robo-counsels to prescribe customized protection plans to a specific client. Clients pick robo-counselors over close to home money related guides because of lower charges, just as customized and aligned proposals.

How to utilize Machine Learning in Finance?

Regardless of the considerable number of points of interest of ML and AI, even organizations with deep pockets frequently experience serious difficulties extricating the genuine incentive from this innovation. Monetary administrations occupants need to misuse the extraordinary chances of ML at the same time, sensibly, they have an obscure thought of how information science functions, and how to utilize it.

Consistently, they experience comparable difficulties, like the absence of business KPIs. This, this way, brings about ridiculous gauges and depletes spending plans. It isn't sufficient to have a reasonable programming foundation set up (although that would be a decent start). It takes an unmistakable vision, strong specialized ability, and assurance to convey an important ML advancement venture.

When you have a decent comprehension of how this innovation will accomplish business targets, continue with thought approval. This is an undertaking for information researchers. They research the thought and help you plan reasonable KPIs and make sensible appraisals.

Note that you need every one of the information gathered now. Else, you would require an information specialist to gather and tidy up this information.

Contingent upon a specific use case and business conditions, monetary organizations can pursue various ways to receive ML. How about we look at them?

Renounce AI and spotlight on enormous information building.

Frequently, monetary organizations start their AI extends to acknowledge they need legitimate information building. Max Nechepurenko, a senior information researcher at N-iX, remarks:

When building up a [data science] arrangement, I'd prompt utilizing the Occam's razor rule, which means not overcomplicating. Most organizations that go for AI, in truth, need to concentrate on strong information designing, applying measurements to the collected information, and representation of that information.

Simply applying factual models to handled and well-organized information would be sufficient for a bank to disconnect different bottlenecks and wasteful aspects in its activities.

What are the instances of such bottlenecks? That could be lines at a particular branch, dull undertakings that can be dispensed with, wasteful HR exercises, blemishes of the versatile banking application, etc.

In addition, the greatest piece of any information science venture comes down to building an organized biological system of stages that gather siloed information from several sources like CRMs, revealing programming, spreadsheets, and that's just the beginning.

Before applying any calculations, you need the information properly organized and tidied up. At exactly that point, you can further transform that information into experiences. ETL (extricating, changing, and stacking) and further cleaning of the information represent around 80% of the AI undertaking's time.

Utilize outsider ML arrangements

Regardless of whether your organization chooses to use ML in its up and coming task, you don't need to grow new calculations and models.

Most ML undertakings manage issues that have just been tended to. Tech goliaths like Google, Microsoft, Amazon, and IBM sell ML programming as an administration.

These out-of-the-crate arrangements are, as of now, prepared to explain different business errands. On the off chance that your task covers a similar use cases, do you accept your group can outflank calculations from these tech titans with goliath R&D focuses?

One genuine model is Google's numerous attachment and-play proposal arrangements. That product applies to different spaces, and it is just consistent to check on whether they fit your business case.

An ML architect can execute the framework concentrating on your particular information and business space. The expert needs to remove the information from various sources, change it to fit for this specific framework, get the outcomes, and picture the discoveries.

The exchange offs are the absence of authority over the outsider framework and constrained arrangement adaptability. Plus, AI calculations don't fit into each utilization case. Ihar Rubanau, a senior information researcher at N-iX remarks:

"An all-inclusive ML algorithm doesn't exist, yet. Information researchers need to alter and tweak calculations before applying them to various business cases crosswise over various areas."

So if a current arrangement from Google comprehends a particular assignment in your specific area, you ought to likely utilize it. If not, go for custom improvement and mix

Development and combination

Building up ML arrangement without any preparation is one of the most dangerous, costliest, and tedious alternatives. In any case, this might be the best way to apply ML innovation to some business cases.

ML innovative work focuses on a special need in a specific specialty, and it requires a top to bottom examination. In the event that there are no prepared to-utilize arrangements that were created to take care of those particular issues, outsider AI programming is probably going to deliver incorrect outcomes. You will most likely need to depend vigorously on the open-source AI libraries from Google and the preferences. Current ML tasks are generally about applying existing best in class libraries to a specific space and use case.

MACHINE LEARNING IN BUSINESS

ML in business helps in upgrading business versatility and improving business tasks for organizations over the globe. Computerized reasoning instruments and various ML calculations have increased colossal fame in the business examination network. Factors, for example, developing volumes, simple accessibility of information, less expensive and quicker computational handling, and moderate information stockpiling have prompted a gigantic ML blast. In this way, associations would now be able to profit by seeing how organizations can utilize AI and execute the equivalent in their procedures.

Employments of Machine Learning in Business

ML helps in separating important data from an enormous arrangement of crude information. Whenever actualized correctly, ML can fill in as an answer for an assortment of business complexities issues, and foresee complex client practices. We have likewise observed a portion of the real innovation monsters, for example, Google, Amazon, Microsoft, and so forth., thinking of their Cloud Machine Learning stages. A portion of the key manners by which ML can help your business are recorded here -

Client Lifetime Value Prediction

Client lifetime esteem forecast and client division are a portion of the real difficulties looked by the advertisers today. Organizations approach a gigantic measure of information, which can be successfully used to infer important business bits of knowledge. ML and information mining can enable organizations to anticipate client practices, acquiring examples, and help in sending most ideal ideas to singular clients in light of their perusing and buy chronicles.

Prescient Maintenance

Assembling firms routinely pursue preventive and restorative support rehearses, which are regularly costly and wasteful. Regardless, with the appearance of ML, organizations in this segment can utilize ML to find important experiences and examples covered up in their processing plant information. This is known as prescient support, and it helps in decreasing the dangers related to unforeseen disappointments and takes out superfluous costs. ML design can be fabricated utilizing authentic information, work process representation apparatus, adaptable investigation condition, and the criticism circle.

Takes out Manual Data Entry

Copy and mistaken information are the absolute most concerning issues looked by THE organizations today. Prescient demonstrating calculations and ML can fundamentally dodge any blunders brought about by manual information passage. ML projects improve these

64

procedures by utilizing the found information. In this way, the workers can use a similar time for completing undertakings that enhance the business.

Recognizing Spam

AI in distinguishing spam has been used for a long while. Already, email specialist co-ops utilized prior, rule-based methods to sift through spam. In any case, spam channels are presently making new manage by utilizing neural systems to identify spam and phishing messages.

Item Recommendations

Unaided learning helps in creating item based suggestion frameworks. The majority of the online business sites today are utilizing AI for making item proposals. Here, the ML calculations utilize the client's buy history and match it with the huge item stock to recognize shrouded examples and gathering comparable items together. These items are then proposed to clients, consequently propelling item buy.

Money related Analysis

With huge volumes of quantitative and precise recorded information, ML would now be able to be utilized in budgetary examination. ML is as of now being utilized in the fund for a portfolio the executives, algorithmic exchanging, advance guaranteeing, and misrepresentation identification. Nonetheless, future uses of ML in the account will incorporate Chatbots and other conversational interfaces for security, client assistance, and assessment examination.

Picture Recognition

Likewise, known as computer vision, picture acknowledgment can create numeric and emblematic data from pictures and other high-dimensional information. It includes information mining, ML, design acknowledgment, and database learning revelation. ML in picture acknowledgment is a significant viewpoint and is utilized by organizations in various businesses including human services, autos, and so on.

Restorative Diagnosis

ML in restorative analysis has assisted a few social insurance associations with improving the patient's wellbeing and lessen medicinal services costs, utilizing prevalent demonstrative instruments and viable treatment plans. It is presently utilized in social insurance to make a practically consummate conclusion, foresee readmissions, suggest meds, and distinguish high-hazard patients. These forecasts and bits of knowledge are drawn utilizing patient records and informational collections alongside the side effects shown by the patient.

Improving Cyber Security

ML can be utilized to build the security of an association as digital security is one of the serious issues unraveled by AI. Here, Ml enables new-age suppliers to assemble more up to date innovations, which rapidly and viably identify obscure dangers.

Expanding Customer Satisfaction

ML can help in improving client dedication and guarantee predominant client experience. This is accomplished by utilizing the past call records for dissecting the client conduct and dependent on that the customer necessity will be accurately relegated to the most appropriate client assistance official. This diminishes the expense and the measure of time put resources into overseeing client relationships. Consequently, real associations utilize prescient calculations to give their clients proposals of items they appreciate.

POINTERS FOR APPLYING MACHINE LEARNING TO BUSINESS PROBLEMS

1 – Begin with a need issue, not a toy issue

In an off-mic discussion with Dr. Charles Martin (AI specialist in the Bay Area), he referenced that numerous organizations read about ML with excitement and choose to "discover some approach to utilize it." This prompts groups without genuine inspiration or energy (or submitted assets) to drive a real outcome. Pick a business issue that issues colossally, and appears to have a high probability of being explained

UBER's Danny Lange has referenced from the stage that there is one manner of thinking that is almost certain to yield productive AI use case thoughts: "On the off chance that we just knew _____."

Ask yourself, what mission-basic business data would you say you are kicking the bucket to know, yet can't as of now get to? Possibly it understands the lead sources destined to yield the most elevated client lifetime esteem, or the client conduct most characteristic of anticipated agitate.

2-You can give it information, yet the majority of the setting must originate from you

Thoroughly considering what data to "feed" your calculation isn't as simple as one may assume. While ML calculations are proficient in recognizing connections, they won't comprehend the realities encompassing the information that may make it applicable or superfluous. Here are a few instances of how "setting" could hinder building up a powerful ML arrangement:

Foreseeing eCommerce client lifetime esteem: A calculation could be given information about recorded client lifetime esteem, without considering that huge numbers of the clients with the most astounding lifetime worth were reached by means of a telephone effort program that kept running for more than two years however neglected to equal the initial investment, in spite of creating new deals. On the off chance that such a phone follow-up program won't be a piece of future eCommerce deals development, at that point, those deals shouldn't have been encouraged to the machine.

Deciding restorative recuperation time: Data may be given to a machine to decide treatment for individuals with first-or severely charred areas. The machine may anticipate that some severe singeing unfortunate casualties will require just as much time as severely charred area exploited people since it doesn't consider the quicker and progressively serious consideration that severely charred area unfortunate casualties got verifiably. The setting was not in the information itself, so the machine essentially expect that subsequent degree consumes mend similarly as quick as a first degree.

Suggesting related items: A proposal motor for an eCommerce retailer over-prescribes a particular item. Analysts find later that this item was advanced intensely over a year back, so chronicled information demonstrated a huge uptick in deals from existing purchasers; nonetheless, these limited-time buys were sold increasingly dependent on the "bargain" and the low cost, and less so by the real related expectation of the client.

3 – Expect to tinker, change, and conform to discover ROI

Building an ML arrangement requires cautious reasoning and testing in choosing calculations, choosing information, cleaning information, and testing in a live domain. There are no "out-of-the-case" AI answers for remarkable and complex business use cases. Notwithstanding for very normal use cases (suggestion motors, anticipating client agitate), every application will fluctuate broadly and require cycle and modification. On the off chance that an organization goes into an ML venture without assets focused on an all-inclusive time of tinkering, it might never accomplish a valuable outcome.

ML doesn't yet appear in a slick box, and worth is created by hard reasoning, exploratory structure, and – now and again – hard science. A smidgen of time on Google and YouTube, and you can get the hang of how to set up DropBox for your business. Anticipating beat rate over your client fragments with AI? Not a similar game.

Planning to get business esteem from ML suggests having the prepared ability, master direction, and a (regularly) huge "information purging" period – and none of it is destined to be a success, as Dr. Martin states appropriately above. In the event that Google, Amazon, and Facebook could get their understudies to set up ML frameworks, would they truly be burning through a great many dollars to scoop the world's top AI ability out of scholastics to work for them?

While ML isn't a simple arrangement, it's additionally not one that any future-disapproved of business can leave off the table for a long time. The efficiencies picked up by the "rockstar" tech organizations through AI are significant, and new companies here in the Bay Area aren't simply getting financed on the grounds that "AI" is a popular expression – it's likewise in light of the fact that a considerable lot of them have an incredible and solid business case.

CHAPTER FOUR
THE IMPACTS OF MACHINE LEARNING

The field of mechanical autonomy has significantly progressed with a few new broad, innovative accomplishments. One is the ascent of enormous information, which offers a greater chance to incorporate programming ability with mechanical frameworks. Another is the utilization of new sorts of sensors and associated gadgets to screen ecological perspectives like temperature, pneumatic force, light, movement, and the sky is the limit from there. The majority of this serves mechanical autonomy and the age of increasingly mind-boggling and advanced robots for some, utilizes, including assembling, wellbeing and security, and human help.

The field of mechanical technology likewise crosses with issues around AI. Since robots are physically discrete units, they are seen to have their very own knowledge, yet one constrained by their programming and abilities. Apply autonomy, Design, development, and utilization of machines (robots) to perform undertakings done customarily by people. Robots are generally utilized in such ventures as vehicle production to perform straightforward redundant assignments, and in businesses where work must be performed in situations dangerous to people. Numerous parts of mechanical technology include human-made consciousness; robots might be furnished with what might be compared to human faculties, for example, vision, contact, and the capacity to detect temperature. Some are even fit for straightforward basic leadership, and ebb and flow mechanical autonomy research is designed for contriving robots with a level of independence that will allow versatility and basic leadership in an unstructured domain. The present mechanical robots don't look like people; a robot in human structure is called an android.

Machining applications experience the ill effects of individual dangers; anyway, these intricacies would now be able to be settled utilizing mechanical innovation. Mechanical automated innovation is inflexible, solid and amazingly solid. Comprising of computerized building, the apparatuses are perfect for molding or boring into hard surfaces like metals. Fast execution and accuracy are specific qualities of automated machining based items. Created to improve stylish and mechanical structure, automated machines having multifaceted geometrics that capacity on computer-based innovation. This implies automated machining requires refined programming and effective EOAT goals.

Mechanical innovation that watches out for apparatus comprises of an adaptable structure and utilization of programming that is introduced in the working region. The programming of automated accuracy machining requires direct capability by specialists (mechanical and computer), which can't offer visual investigation, however is time productive. Utilizing dependable mechanical machining based items has certainly improved the standard nature of production and guaranteed budgetary protection.

The Impacts of Machine Learning Advancements

AI has effectively positively shaped social insurance just as a misrepresentation location, with PayPal utilizing it to battle against illegal tax avoidance. What's more, both new and rising AI advances are set to cause a ripple effect in the domains of promoting. These present advancements include:

IBM Watson

A supercomputer that joins ML with unrivaled logical programming, IBM Watson is a completely enhanced inquiry noting framework - and it forms at a pace of 80 teraflops (trillion drifting point activities for every second).

Flash

Focusing on the universe of enrolment, Spark is a stage that can prescribe the best possibility for empty jobs utilizing a modern calculation. By including a large group of prerequisites, attributes, and inclinations, Spark's installed application addresses other programming and returns the best possibility to organizations arranged by appropriateness.

Kafka

An ML arrangement, Kafka Apache enables brands and organizations to assemble continuous information gushing applications or pipelines to complete basic capacities or translate data from an assortment of sources. It's as of now utilized by LinkedIn to deal with more than 1.4 trillion messages for every day, increment proficiency, and help them settle on basic choices dependent on smart information.

MACHINE LEARNING ISN'T JUST FOR ADVANCED FIRST ORGANIZATIONS

An ongoing report proposes that chatbots resolution 85% of client care connections by 2020. As the predominance of AI turns out to be progressively pervasive in the business world, any semblance of Netflix, among others, are putting vigorously in ML innovation with the end goal of expanding client commitment.

In any case, this front line innovation is never again selective to ML scientists and advanced organizations like Amazon and Google. On the off chance that effectively used, it can affect key regions of the promoting enormous information environment in 2018.

With the keen capacity to mechanize client care connections in a shrewd, human manner, chatbots serve to build profitability in a major manner. 44% of shoppers in the US as of now lean toward chatbots to people for client relations - a demonstration of the viability of ML innovation for business.

By democratizing the utilization of key information and examination, giving staff at the forefront, just as those in specialized and promoting jobs, with the fundamental aptitudes, business pioneers won't just take full advantage of ML innovation yet help empower appropriation all through the business.

Anyway, how precisely would businesses be able to utilize ML to expand profitability and effectiveness?

Computerized information representation

90% of the world's information was created over the most recent two years alone. The capacity to picture eminent connections in information enables organizations to settle on better choices, yet also manufactures certainty. Various devices offer rich previews of information that can be applied to both organized and unstructured information. Be that as it may, at present, representation apparatuses are just incredible if you can translate the fundamental information.

As ML creates, we hope to see more easy to understand information mechanized perception stages and gadgets that are orchestrated and deciphered through AI, giving an abundance of new bits of knowledge, expanding efficiency simultaneously.

Content Management and Analysis

One of the most basic approaches to support brand awareness, drive commitment, and produce durable shopper connections is by starting significant discussions with your objective client base. As brands and organizations try to participate in progressively significant exchanges with their clients, AI will be basic in breaking down specific words, phrases, expressions, sentences, and substance designs that reverberate with an explicit group of spectator's individuals.

Take Pinterest as a brand effectively utilizing this system to customize recommendations to clients. By preparing 150 million pictures to look through every month, it utilizes ML to help source content that clients will be keen on dependent on items they have just stuck. It likewise takes a gander at subtitles from stuck substance and which things get stuck to the equivalent virtual sheets to interface a specific pair of pants to a shirt stuck close by it, regardless of them looking nothing indistinguishable.

This year and past, ML will incite a movement in the lexical examination, enabling advertisers to customize their substance at a battle just as an individual level, to inconceivably improve commitment.

Gradual Machine Learning

By utilizing huge and complex arrangements of information, ML instruments can build up their insight base and capacities on a progressing premise, helping a business to wind up more intelligent, savvier, and increasingly educated through mechanization.

At present, how ML stages translate prescient information can be to some degree restricted, missing pieces of key information subsequently. Be that as it may, as steady ML advances, arrangements will be made that permits new improvements and layers of information to be taken off progressively, improving prescient capacities and promoting execution, therefore. Improved precision with no vast gaps in information means better outcomes and gradual ML will assume a crucial job in that.

As ML turns out to be progressively common, increasingly received, and all the more broadly utilized, brands and organizations will have the option to utilize its capacity to further their potential benefit, seeing how it can yield promoting results and quicken development. As opposed to supplanting existing jobs, ML will expand them, executing human endeavors as opposed to ruining them.

Presently ML is grabbing genuine energy; it's the duty of top-level administrators to guide their organization the correct way, guaranteeing each group sees how ML will extend and improve their jobs.

This new and energizing innovation will help make organizations progressively gainful, prescient, productive, and shrewd; however from the start, it might be met with a specific degree of skepticism.

By contemplating what you need these ML substances to do, how we need them to act, or work and how you are getting down to business with them to drive the business forward, you will have the option to reveal a straightforward system, helping other people adjust their abilities and procedures likewise.

To effectively actualize ML into the work environment, advanced pioneers must think about three basic stages:

Portrayal: Collecting information in databases to take a gander at past bits of knowledge and assemble a well-characterized preview of the business' points, objectives, and prerequisites.

Expectation: Gathering prescient information to anticipate basic future results for the business. To guarantee this is done effectively, officials must guarantee the quality, lucidity, and association of this information is immaculate.

Remedy: This piece of the ML appropriation procedure will take the most man-machine collective methodology. To decipher these comprehensive floods of information and use them to see how the business ought to work inside its new biological system, the C-suite ought to be straightforwardly engaged with the creation and definition of the goals that these calculations endeavor to upgrade.

We're entering a reality where individuals and machines will work in concordance to interface, crusade, and market their items and administrations such that is increasingly close to home, effective and educated than at any other time.

By grasping the capability of ML, getting into the correct outlook and helping your group see how it can enable them to carry out their responsibilities all the more adequately, you remain to have a genuine effect tomorrow and long into what's to come.

KEY CONSIDERATIONS AND IMPLICATIONS

The ethical segment — The degree of knowledge and "Deep quality" that a machine applies is an immediate aftereffect of the information it gets. One result is that, in light of the information input, machines may prepare themselves to neutralize the enthusiasm of certain people or be one-sided. Inability to delete inclination from a machine calculation may deliver results that are not under the ethical benchmarks of society. However, not all analysts, researchers, and specialists accept that ML will be terrible to society. Some accept that ML can be created to reflect the human mind and get human moralistic brain science to improve society.

The precision of hazard appraisals — Risk evaluations are utilized in numerous regions of society to assess and quantify the potential dangers that might be engaged with explicit situations. The expanding notoriety of utilizing ML hazard appraisals to settle on significant choices for individuals is an immediate aftereffect of the developing trust among people and machines. Be that as it may, there are not kidding suggestions to note when utilizing an ML framework to make chance evaluations. A quantitative expert gauges that some ML procedures may flop up to 90 percent when tried in a genuine setting. The reason is that while calculations utilized in ML depend on a practically unbounded measure of things, a lot of this information is fundamentally the same as. For these machines, finding an example would be simple, yet finding an example that will fit each genuine situation would be troublesome.

Straightforwardness of calculations — Supporters of making straightforwardness in ML advocate for the production of a common and controlled database that isn't in control of anyone element that can control the information; be that as it may, there are numerous reasons why companies are not empowering this. While straightforwardness might be the answer for making trust among clients and machines, not all clients of AI see an advantage there.

Next, we feature a portion of the manners in which these suggestions happen in a few businesses.

SPOTLIGHT: INDUSTRY IMPLICATIONS

Today, ML makes it conceivable to anticipate the probability of a coronary episode with much preferable exactness over previously. While manual frameworks can make the right expectations with around 30 percent precision, an AI calculation made at Carnegie Mellon University had the option to raise the forecast exactness to 80 percent. In an emergency clinic, an 80 percent expectation hypothetically would give a doctor four hours to mediate before the event of the perilous occasion.

Be that as it may, the precision of hazard appraisals in the therapeutic field may differ contingent upon the degree of inclination in the exploration used to prepare the AI calculation. For example, most coronary illness research is directed on men, even though cardiovascular failure indications among people vary in some significant ways. On the off chance that the framework is prepared to perceive respiratory failure side effects found in men, the exactness of anticipating a coronary episode in ladies reduces and may bring about a casualty. Hence, individuals who are influenced by choices dependent on ML hazard appraisals will need to know how these choices are methodically made.

Mutual funds, which have consistently depended intensely on computers to discover drifts in money related information, are progressively advancing toward ML. They will likely have the option to naturally perceive changes in the market and respond rapidly in manners quant models can't. The majority of these calculations are restrictive, which is as it should be. The danger of having straightforwardness for this situation is that as one store ends up fruitful utilizing a specific algorithm, others will need to impersonate that organization's AI technique, reducing everybody's prosperity and making a fake market condition. Consequently, any guideline that endeavors to control the straightforwardness of AI must be reasonable and suitable to the different situations where AI is utilized.

The U.S. National Highway Traffic Safety Administration as of late discharged rules for independent vehicles, requiring automobile producers to willfully present their structure, improvement, testing and arrangement designs before going to advertise with their vehicles. In spite of these endeavors to build the straightforwardness around "the minds" conveyed in self-governing vehicles, vehicle makers, tech organizations and automobile parts producers are in a tight challenge to build up the product behind self-driving autos, and their need to hold advancement endeavors hush-hush to pick up market bit of leeway may wind up harming the fate of independence.

Likewise, the nature of ML itself makes it extremely hard to demonstrate that self-governing vehicles will work securely. Customary computer coding is composed to meet wellbeing necessities and after that, tried to check if it was effective; be that as it may, ML enables a computer to learn and perform at its very own pace and level of multifaceted nature. The more automakers are happy to be straightforward about the information they contribute to the learning calculations, the simpler it will be for legislators and auto wellbeing controllers to make laws that will guarantee the security of purchasers.

CHAPTER FIVE
THE MOST POWERFUL MACHINE LEARNING TECHNIQUES IN DATA MINING

Propelled ML systems are at the nexus of informatics in each industry and field of request, and information mining is among the most concentrated territories of center in the wide field of ML today. Information mining methods incorporate calculations, for example, order, choice tree, neural systems, and relapse, to give some examples. In this area, we investigate information mining systems top to bottom and spread the most significant strategies now at the center of big business innovative work.

Characterization and irregularity location calculations empower us to discover examples and find learning in information which we couldn't see previously. The pertinence of these rising fields to the development and improvement of business and science is boundless. Astounding new domains of information investigation are opening up all over. Without a doubt, the invasion of Big Data related common sense AI instruments make such revelations conceivable. We will take a gander at how relapse calculations work practically speaking and hypothesis, utilizing Python to delineate our models. En route, we will study the rundown of rich strategies for information mining with regards to Big Data suppliers like Quandl, AWS, Socrata, and UCI, all of which give APIs to researching the endless new universe of data mining and ML.

Information mining accentuates the utilization of colossal informational indexes, and the prevalent programming model MapReduce advanced from the unprecedented necessities of using Big Data through concentrated relapse models or neural systems, which frequently contain a large number of AI highlights. Hadoop is an open-source usage of MapReduce from Apache, which encourages the utilization of Big Data in information mining with bunches of processors. Shrewd information portrayal strategies utilize immense databases, for example, DNA sequencing information from the Human Genome Project to find the structures of proteins and encourage robotization of new sedate revelation. A propelled MLalgorithm can foresee whether a particle will tie to a protein target, in this manner anticipating precisely competitor atoms for new sedates! How about we investigate the techniques utilized in such development.

Our voyage into development will interpret best into the most famous language for utilizing AI libraries: Python. Heap Python libraries like SciKit-Learn contain both ML capacities and datasets prepared for preparing and testing. ML code includes complex math, and we need not convoluted issues by beginning in a language with muddled sentence structure; Python is least demanding to peruse, troubleshoot, and run. Python likewise underpins numerous information structures, which make overseeing enormous informational collections simpler. What's more, Python is particularly simple to use for information composing. In a perfect world, to pursue this introduction, feel free to introduce Python on your framework.

The most effortless approach to introduce Python is to give the Anaconda dispersion a chance to arrange every one of the libraries and conditions, just as setting a framework way. Boa constrictor incorporates every one of the libraries we will use here, for example, Scikit-Learn, Pandas, and the center math libraries like Numpy. Another incredible library to encourage the advancement of calculations in Python is the Jupyter Notebook, a freeware system that empowers coding, running, and commenting on Python in your program. The cleanest approach to utilize Python is spot on the order line or terminal. You can begin Python and model lines of code there, and after that, glue them to your preferred manager or IDE. Like this of working prompts commonality with the association of Python parts in your framework.

Boa constrictor is a somewhat enormous establishment record, and on the off chance that you incline toward a less fatty download, basically, get a duplicate of Python from the association, and after that, pip introduces just the libraries required in this introduction. For instance, after refreshing your framework way to incorporate Python, you can run python - m pip introduce jupyter on the order line, or terminal and Jupyter will auto introduce. At that point you can likewise run it from the direction line with the order jupyter scratchpad. As you will find, Jupyter note pads (recently called "iPython") are an exceptionally helpful method for creating ML code and remarking inline to encourage your investigation.

Grasping the Math

Unavoidably, ML in information mining is a scientific undertaking. Framework tasks are the center of the neural system structure. This is valid for two reasons. "Neural systems" are spoken to by frameworks of conditions, and the parameters or coefficients of these conditions establish the components of a grid. These parameters are the "neurons" alluded to in the similarity to the cerebrum. Furthermore, in this manner, most information structures utilized in AI and information mining are demonstrated as frameworks, vectors, or tensors, most generally alluded to as exhibits. The numerically recorded exhibit gives us computational access to the components of clusters to encourage count.

We should confront the math on the off chance that we are going to fathom the crucial ideas of ML genuinely. Although Python and libraries like TensorFlow make it conceivable to do AI without seeing how it functions, we will test further. From perusing and wrangling a dataset right to multivariate straight relapse, some libraries crunch the numbers for you. You can without much of a stretch, pursue an instructional exercise and run an information characterization calculation, yet this won't prompt understanding. We will infiltrate further and take a gander at the center of the reactor!

We are going to apply ML and assemble a prescient model to decide the odds that a patient will end up diabetic dependent on information about weight and other information highlights. Numerous acquaintances with information mining sit around idly on speculations; we're going to assemble a genuine prescient model at present. To start with, we are going to step forward and read a diabetes dataset into a Python cluster! This will develop genuine information about the math mechanics of information mining and ML.

As a fundamental advance, open another Jupyter Notebook. Make an organizer for your new undertaking and open a direct line. At the brief, type jupyter scratchpad, and Jupyter will open in another tab in your default program (obviously, you can pursue this model in your preferred editorial manager without Jupyter). Look back at your order line, and you will see Jupyter producing a ton of programmed discourse there, some of which can be valuable analytically. We should feel free to import the libraries we will require for our model:

1. **import numpy as np**
2. **import pandas as PD**
3. **import matplotlib**
4. **from sklearn import datasets, linear_model**

Here we import Numpy, a Python library which in a split second, gives us incredible control over information structures like that of Octave and MATLAB. This is the thing that we will use to deal with straight variable based math and lattice activities. Pandas is a library intended for DataFrame investigation and supports numerous tasks comparative in usefulness to the spreadsheets of MS Excel, for example, rotate tables. Matplotlib is generally utilized for 2D plotting of information and capacities. What's more, SKLearn is the well-known Python library for ML capacities, which likewise contains numerous datasets for preparing and testing models.

The subsequent stage is to peruse our dataset into a cluster. In this model, we will utilize a diabetes dataset from an examination study openly accessible to foresee the movement of ailment in patients. This is the kind of dataset ordinarily curated on Big Data locales like Quandl and UCI. This specific dataset will fill a few needs for our exhibit. In your Jupyter note pad or editorial manager, enter the accompanying code to peruse in the diabetes dataset:

1. **ds = datasets.load_diabetes()**
2. **X = ds.data**
3. **y = ds.target**
4. **np.shape(X)**

Straight Regression – A First Model

The following stage in our voyage is to construct a model to foresee the sickness movement is an example of patients. The highlights accessible for our model can appear in Table by incorporating age, sex, weight, circulatory strain, and six blood serum tests. The arrangement is to fit a regression model to anticipate the objective incentive in the dataset, which appeared as "Reaction y" in the table. For information perception, we will utilize the weight include (BMI).

94

Feel free to enter the accompanying code to lessen the X exhibit to section 2 (this is a zero list cluster). We use lattice administrators here to isolate the dataset into 362 preparing tests and 80 more for the test:

1. **X = X[:,2]**
2. **X = X.reshape(-1, 1)**
3. **y = y.reshape(-1, 1)**
4. **X_train = X[: -80]**
5. **y_train = y[: -80]**
6. **X_test = X[-80:]**
7. **y_test = y[-80:]**

Presently the dataset is prepared to run a regression. We use SKLearn capacities to prepare the model in the accompanying code:

1. **linear_reg = linear_model.LinearRegression ()**
2. **linear_reg.fit(X_train , y_train)**

```
In [6]:  linear_reg = linear_model.LinearRegression ()
         linear_reg.fit(X_train , y_train)
         linear_reg.score X_test , y_test)

Out[6]:  0.36469910696163765
```

If you are building this model in Jupyter you should see this:

What's more, check the score against the test information like this:

1. **linear_reg.score(X_test , y_test)**

If you are tracking within your editorial manager, you ought to get an outcome around .365 for the test score. This is a crude expectation dependent on a solitary component, the patient weight. With expanding highlight multifaceted nature, we can accomplish better exactness. SciKit-Learn additionally gives the Support Vector Regression to the nonlinear or polynomial fitting of information.

Applied Machine Learning Techniques

Underneath the outside of SKLearn a regression model is enhanced by modifying the parameters to fit the preparation information to the objective result. There is a cost capacity which is limited by a technique, for example, slope drop to fit the preparation information to the known results generally precisely. In the field of information mining, there are numerous well-known varieties and methodologies, for example, calculated relapse. How does this work precisely?

In regression, we take a lot of straight conditions that we work from the highlights in our dataset and settle it for a lot of parameters, which we improve with a cost capacity. Take, for example, we have 442 samples patients, and each sample has ten highlights including sex, age, weight, and blood test outcomes. To set this up as a lot of straight conditions, we compose it in a structure this way:

$$a_{11}x_1 + a_{12}x_2 + a_{13}x_3 = b1$$
$$a_{21}x_1 + a_{22}x_2 + a_{23}x_3 = b2$$
$$a_{31}x_1 + a_{32}x_2 + a_{33}x_3 = b1$$

Wherein each column models the information for a patient. Presently here is the stunt: we know the qualities for X. They are the information includes in the preparation set. Each time we run an instructional course we put the information into the X esteems and enhance the parameters or coefficients. What we need to enhance are the qualities for the coefficients, the a11, a12 ... an. For our situation, the subscripts go up to 10 since we have 10 highlights in the information. 442 columns are going somewhere near 10 highlights going over. So the last parameter in our arrangement of conditions looks like a442 10 in the figure above.

The "target" values are the known qualities in the preparation and test information. They educate us regarding the genuine infection movement in this model. Once more, qualities are what we need to "explain" for or enhance utilizing a strategy of AI called relapse. To bring up a couple of more things of prominent language tossed about freely in articles about AI, the "layers" of a "neural system" are the quantity of parameters opposite left to directly in the above conditions. Qualities are the "neurons," which are "actuated" when the model is "prepared." So as should be obvious the frequently utilized similarity to the human cerebrum is a freely fitting relationship to be sure.

The following stage in setting up an AI model is to modify this arrangement of conditions as a lattice or set of frameworks. We can do this by composing qualities in their very own grid like this:

$$
\begin{bmatrix} a_{11} & a_{12} & \cdots & a_{1n} \\ a_{21} & a_{22} & \cdots & a_{2n} \\ \vdots & \vdots & \ddots & \vdots \\ a_{m1} & a_{m2} & \cdots & a_{mn} \end{bmatrix} \begin{pmatrix} x_1 \\ x_2 \\ \vdots \\ x_n \end{pmatrix} = \begin{pmatrix} b_1 \\ b_2 \\ \vdots \\ b_m \end{pmatrix}
$$

Presently here we have something that Python and particularly Numpy realize how to process proficiently! Here likewise, you can perceive any reason why a total arrangement of information is significant to the arrangement. If one of the a qualities is missing, at that point we get into one more method of information mining which has the objective of assessing missing information.

The answer for the above conditions is a procedure of setting up a cost capacity and limiting the expense by changing the a qualities until the b esteems most intently coordinate the objective qualities in our preparation set. The SKLearn library does this computation for us. When the preparation information is utilized to locate the ideal parameters, we, at that point test the model by utilizing the test esteems to score the precision of the model.

Intersection the Finish Line

Although this is a direct arrangement, there is a comparative technique for dealing with nonlinear information displaying. Engineers, for the most part, yield a diagram demonstrating a dissipate plot of focuses with a line down the center of the information indicating how the model approximates the objective information. Like the "neural system" similarity to the human cerebrum, this information perception is just a relationship, and it might deceive. A shortsighted representation of our model can be produced with this code:

1. **plt.scatter(X_test , y_test)**
2. **plt.plot(X_test , linear_reg.predict(X_test))**
3. **plt.show ()**

The outcome, when we do a trillion cycles over a million parameters, doesn't fit perfectly on a MATPLOTLIB outline. This is the reason we get astonishing and in some cases, baffling outcomes, some keen thoughts and others which recommend we include determination and how that affects the outcomes. This nonlinear regularly erratic part of a model planned to anticipate is the thing that contains a trace of particular knowledge.

THE DIFFERENCE BETWEEN DATA MINING AND MACHINE LEARNING

Data mining is the testing of accessible datasets to distinguish examples and inconsistencies. AI is the procedure of machines (a.k.a. PCs) gaining from heterogeneous information such that impersonates the human learning process. The two ideas together empower both past information portrayal and future information forecast.

There are Many Lenses of Data Mining

The motivation behind data mining is to distinguish designs in information, and examples can be recognized from numerous points of view contingent upon what data is required.

1) Data mining is utilized to order information.

Ordering data is something we perform once a day, similar to when we sort clothing and separate shirts, pants, socks, and so forth. As far as large information, arranging winds up unmistakably increasingly entangled. For instance, credit checks get to an individual's monetary history. In the wake of incorporating information on existing obligations, salary, and late installment narratives, advance candidates are arranged into either "qualified" or "ineligible."

2) Data mining is utilized to distinguish the relationship in the information.

For instance, consider a market that sets up an internet shopping framework with a virtual shopping basket. When information is gathered from a large number of clients, it would likely be uncovered that individuals who purchase sausages regularly purchase buns and ketchup also, or that individuals who add pasta noodles to their trucks frequently purchase pasta sauce.

As another model, consider an application that gathers phone GPS area information from its clients.

Utilizing data mining, experts can reason that a couple of individuals, call them Rachel, Ross, Joey, Chandler, and Monica, assemble each day at about a similar time at a bistro called Central Perk (those of you that watched "Companions" recognize what this is about). By that, they can surmise that Rachel, Ross, Joey, Chandler, and Monica are companions.

3) Data mining is utilized to distinguish exceptions and irregularities.

Distinguishing strange data can be helpful. A model would be a misrepresentation location framework kept running by a Visa organization. On the off chance that out of the blue, high-ticket thing

101

buys are produced using a person's record, and those buys are outside their home state, security projects will confine the episode and ring virtual alerts to show something unordinary is occurring that warrants further examination, for example, a stop on the record and a telephone call to the client. Another model, considering the Central Perk situation above, would be if it was seen that Chandler and Monica quit coming to Central Perk by and large in the wake of being steadfast individuals for a long time. A pattern that is broken proposes that something has changed, which is, in reality, obvious – Chandler and Monica got hitched and moved to suburbia.

4) Data mining is utilized to amass information.

Bunch investigation bunches things together dependent on shared properties. For instance, if scholars are given the DNA groupings of 1,000 unique species, calculations that think about the successions may bunch the species into five general gatherings that are upon examination recognized as warm-blooded creatures, reptiles, creatures of land and water, fowls, and fish.

5) Data mining is utilized to perform a relapse investigation and create forecast models.

Regression investigation looks to examine the connection between quantitative factors. Computing private land esteems an ideal case of relapse examination. Private land costs are affected by various variables, including area, the number of beds/showers, the populace of the city, separation to schools, and so forth. On the off chance that the information from several as of late sold properties is gathered and broke down, information mining could decide how much each factor adds to the price tag. Utilizing that data, land speculators would then be able to anticipate esteems and patterns. Both land financial specialists and insurance agencies depend vigorously on such prescient models.

Regardless of the kind of data mining, all information mining systems have a definitive objective of removing designs from the information.

Data researchers are not simply keen on portraying existing information, even though that is an enormous aspect of their responsibilities. They are similarly keen on foreseeing future data and precisely portraying obscure data. ML is a way that data mining yield is utilized to produce devices that can be applied to novel data.

Considerations of Using Data in Real-Time

Before dashing off to your work area and coding up a continuous application that outputs the whole Twitter firehose, it merits considering if ongoing is the best approach. Because constant preparing is accessible doesn't mean you ought to consistently utilize it.

Finance related administrations organizations utilize continuous handling for applications that help supporters choose whether to play out an exchange on a stock; the choice to purchase or to sell must be registered in milliseconds. In this unique situation, information that is considered "old"— anything longer than 10 or 20 seconds—does not merit preparing when you consider what number of exchanges may have happened from different dealers. The cost could have changed ordinarily inside that length.

Then again, a web-based business webpage utilizing AI to produce proposals for clients could clump up a few exchanges and procedure them occasionally every 3, 6, 12, or even 24 hours. Clustering up bigger volumes of exchanges has certain points of interest. Section 10 spreads clump preparing in more detail. More up to date handling frameworks utilize in-memory preparing, which requires no moderate, customary optional information store and deters the conventional concentrate, change, and burden (ETL) as found in customary SQL-based business knowledge frameworks.

Another thought is capacity volume: Is it important to store every one of the information? Will putting away the prepared information do the trick for your motivation? Or then again, will you have to store the starting point information for further preparing later? The facts confirm that the expense of capacity is diminishing (Moore's Law), however capacity still has real cost suggestions that you should consider. In what manner will the information be put away? Where will it be put away? On the off chance that the information will be put away on the cloud (on Amazon S3 cans, for instance), at that point, are there protection worries that you should address? Have you thought about the information wellbeing (reinforcements and re-establish administration levels) and information security (protection, mystery, and access control) for the data?

With the expanding rate of figuring, the diving cost of capacity, and the some superior, minimal effort database frameworks accessible, there is nothing to prevent you from utilizing a few information stores for future handling. You can consider a conventional social database, for example, MySQL, a section stores, for example, HBase, and a chart database, for example, Neo4J or Apache Giraffe. Consider your information lifecycle, use cases, and the qualities/motivation behind each SQL and NoSQL framework inside your span

POTENTIAL USES FOR A REAL-TIME SYSTEM

The uses of a constant information framework are wide and extensive. With the extending volume of significant online life and portable information, it's winding up progressively significant for ongoing frameworks to empower moment availability and suggestions for individuals in any place they are. Area-based focused on promoting is a decent contender for the ongoing investigation. Such a framework must search for offers dependent on the area of the client's gadget, notwithstanding the continuous setting of the client's circumstance (for instance, climate, traffic, time of day, day of the year, and neighborhood, breaking news).

Finance related exchanging has recently been referenced as a possibility for ongoing preparing. Organizations are putting intensely into ongoing calculations that can exchange at incredibly high speeds (microseconds) utilizing algorithmic exchanging to figure and perform a large number of exchanges every second. Various calculations can be utilized for these estimations. A few frameworks consider news features and Twitter channels, and after that, they exchange on the assessment of the story. Such frameworks have changing degrees of achievement. Installments and extortion recognition calculations can examine exchanges progressively and banner dangerous exchanges as they occur. As handling force expands, organizations can hold onto more factors, for example, past client exchanges, area, and buy conduct between snaps in delicate ongoing.

In situations where an intuitive reaction to an end client or framework is required, a continuous framework merits considering. In such cases, keeping information only in memory speeds things up impressively. Optional capacity ought to be utilized distinctly to speed recuperation, restarting the memory framework, and if more inside and out preparing is required over bigger informational indexes.

To more readily comprehend parts of the present ML/AI insurgency, it is helpful to think about the chosen foundation and terms about the field. Artificial intelligence as a field of study has been around since the center 1950s; nonetheless, it is the ongoing development in information accessibility, calculations, and registering power that have carried resurgence to the field, particularly for ML dependent on profound learning neural systems (DLNN). Practically speaking, it has turned out to be critical to recognize the expression "simulated intelligence," that is currently most normally connected with having machines accomplish explicit errands inside a tight area or control, from the expression "counterfeit general insight" (AGI) that exemplifies the first and advanced objective of having machines carry on as people do. The previous is in the present, while the last is likely past predictable skylines.

ML has, for quite some time, been utilized for non-direct relapse, to discover designs in information, and filled in as one methodology for accomplishing AI objectives. Three sorts of learning are usually perceived as "regulated" where the framework gains from known information; "unaided" where the unassisted framework discovers designs in information; and, "fortification" realizing where the framework is customized to make arrangements and is "compensated" here and there for right answers, however, is offered no direction about erroneous answers. Each of the three modes is utilized at the present boondocks.

For the reasons for this section, "information science" is a general term that infers deliberate obtaining and examination, speculation testing, and forecast around the information. The field along these lines envelops wide-running parts of the data advances utilized in information obtaining, combination, mining, estimating, and basic leadership. For instance, all parts of information science would be utilized for self-sufficient frameworks. On the other hand, materials "informatics" are centered around the investigation of materials information to adjust its structure and to locate the best utilization of the data; for example, materials informatics is a subset of materials information science. Information sciences, informatics, and some ML advancements are identified with one another, and specifically were utilized in research and designing for over 50 years. In any case, until the most recent decade, their effect was negligible on materials and procedures improvement, structures designing, or the test techniques utilized for parameterizing and checking models. The difficulties in MPSE are essentially excessively intricate and information was excessively restricted and costly to get. Presently, ponders do demonstrate that the ML advancements can discover connections, at times find physical laws, and propose practical structures that may somehow or another be covered up to normal logical examination. However, these are not many.

Verifiable endeavors in ML endeavored employments of "artificial neural systems" (ANN or NN) to impersonate the neural associations and data handling comprehended to happen in human cerebrums (organic neural systems or BNN). In a manner that freely mirrors the human cerebrum, these systems comprise of scientific structures that characterize complex, non-direct connections between information data and yields. By and large, for all system learning techniques, the ANN contains layers of hubs (lattices) that hold prepared information that was changed by the useful relationship that associates the hubs. A given hub gets weighted contributions from a past layer, plays out an activity to change a net weight, and passes the outcome to the following layer. This is finished by shaping enormous networks of over and over-applied numerical capacities/changes associating hubs, and extension of highlights at every hub. To utilize the system, one utilizes "preparing information" of known relationship to the ideal yields, to "educate" the systems about the connections between known data sources and good yields (the loads). By cycle of the preparation information, the systems "learn" to allocate fitting weighting components to the numerical activities (straight, sigmoidal, and so forth.) that make the associations, and to discover both solid and feeble connections inside information.

Critically, the early organizes regularly had just one-to-three shrouded layers between the info and yield layers, and a predetermined number of associations between "neurons;" in this manner, they were not all that valuable for AI-based basic leadership. As of not long ago, PCs

110

didn't have the limit, and calculations were immature to allow any more profound systems or critical advancement on enormous scale difficulties. The methods missed the mark regarding the present profound learning devices associated with AI basic leadership. Thus, with a couple of exemptions, the authentic specialized methodologies for accomplishing AI, even inside explicit applications, have been difficultly attached to "rules," requiring human specialists to depict and refresh the guidelines for regularly growing use cases and learned occasions—that is up to this point.

As a rule, the present ANN has changed totally. The accessibility of immense measures of computerized information for preparing; enhancements to calculations that license new organize structures, prepared preparing, and even self-educating; and parallel handling and development in figuring force including illustrations processor unit (GPU) and tensor handling unit (TPU) models have all prompted profound learning neural systems DLNN or "profound learning" (DL). Such DLNN frequently contain tens-to-thousands of concealed layers, as opposed to the authentic one-to-three layers (hence the expression "profound learning"). These propelled systems can contain a billion hubs or more and a lot more associations between hubs. Setting this into point of view, the human cerebrum is assessed to contain on the request for 100-to-1000 trillion associations (neurotransmitters) between under 100 billion neurons. By examination, the present best profound systems are as yet 4–5 sets of extent littler than a human mind. In any case, BNN still fills in as models for the structures being investigated, and being just 4–5 sets of greatness littler than a human BNN still gives huge, uncommon abilities.

Inside DL advancements, there are a few use-case-subordinate models and executions that give amazing ways to deal with various AI spaces. Those dependent on DLNN ordinarily require broad informational collections for preparing (several thousand to a large number of clarified occurrences for preparing). As referenced beforehand, this introduces a noteworthy test for their utilization in MPSE that, in all likelihood, should be alleviated utilizing recreated information in advantageous interaction with the tentatively obtained information. "Convolutional and de-convolutional or all the more fittingly transposed convolutional neural systems" (CNN and TCNN, individually) and their varieties have three significant system engineering properties including 3D volumes of hub exhibits and profound layers of these clusters, neighborhood availability to such an extent that solitary a couple of 10s of hubs speak with one another at once, and shared loads for every unit of associated hubs. These traits profoundly accelerate preparing, allowing the extremely significant more noteworthy profundities. During use, the numerical convolution (transposed convolution) activity permits simultaneous taking in and utilization of data from the majority of the locally thin, however profound cluster components. Compositionally, the systems generally emulate the BNN of the human eye, and have demonstrated their adequacy in picture acknowledgment and grouping assignments, presently routinely beating human execution in a few undertakings.

A few much further developed DLNN structures rose as of late including "Repetitive" (RNN) that have taken on restored utility in their utilization for solo language interpretation, "Territorial" (R-CNN) utilized for picture object identification, and "Generative Adversarial Networks" (GAN) for unaided learning and preparing information decrease, to give some examples. Every one of these models adjusts DL to various errand spaces. For instance, language interpretation and discourse acknowledgment advantage by including a type of memory for time arrangement examination (RNN). GAN incorporates re-enacted in addition to solo preparing, or S + U learning, for which reproduced information is "redressed" utilizing genuine unlabeled information. Fortification learning innovation, of which GAN is a subset, was utilized for the self-educated machine that aced "Go" and has been utilized for the latest language interpretation techniques. Further, in any undertaking that has likenesses to parts of MPSE, S + U preparing was utilized to address facial acknowledgment frameworks for the impacts of posture changes, simply from re-enacted information. Given the generally extending uses of DL, there is a high probability that structures, calculations, and techniques for preparing will keep on advancing quickly throughout the following 3–5 years.

Maybe the most testing objective for ML/AI techniques is to proceed with the extension of independent frameworks, particularly for MPSE innovative work. Gradually, these frameworks are advancing into life sciences, sedate disclosure, and the quest for new practical materials.

ML empowered advancement in materials structure disclosure doesn't of-and-to-itself infer dominance of the handling and microstructure configuration space. For these last plan difficulties, new self-ruling instruments are required, to a great extent, dependent on imaging sciences being better coupled to high-throughput experimentation, which showed the intensity of programmed classifiers for organic pictures. Moreover, given the advances in profound learning and publicly supporting utilized for clarifying the picture and video information, maybe the seeds have been sewn for long-run improvement of frameworks to self-governing outline for materials information while keeping them consistently refreshed. One may conceive that when joined with DL for PC vision, long-extend improvements should allow independent materials portrayal, and at last to the authority of materials various leveled microstructure for new materials plan through self-sufficient microstructure search.

CHAPTER SIX
UTILIZING AI AND DECISION TREE FOR SENTIMENT ANALYSIS

Assumption examination computationally gets from a composed book utilizing the author's disposition (regardless of whether positive, negative, or impartial), close to the content theme. This sort of investigation demonstrates valuable for individuals working in showcasing and correspondence since it causes them to comprehend what clients and buyers think about an item or administration and along these lines, demonstration properly (for example, attempting to recoup unsatisfied clients or choosing to utilize an alternate deal system). Everybody performs estimation investigation. For instance, when perusing content, individuals normally attempt to decide the feeling that moved the individual who composed it. Notwithstanding, when the quantity of writings to peruse and comprehend is excessively tremendous, and the content continually gathers, as in web-based life and client messages, mechanizing assessment investigation is significant.

The forthcoming model is a trial of RNNs utilizing Keras and TensorFlow that manufactures an assumption examination calculation fit for grouping the dispositions communicated in a film audit. The information is an example of the IMDb dataset that contains 50,000 audits (split down the middle among train and test sets) of motion pictures joined by a mark communicating the conclusion of the survey

116

(0=negative, 1=positive). IMDb is an enormous online database containing data about movies, TV arrangement, and computer games. Initially kept up by a fan base, it's presently kept running by an Amazon auxiliary. On IMDb, individuals discover the data they need about their preferred show just as post their remarks or compose a survey for different guests to peruse.

Keras offers a downloadable wrapper for IMDb information. You get ready, mix, and orchestrate this information into a train and a test set. Specifically, the IMDb printed information offered by Keras is rinsed of accentuation, standardized into lowercase, and changed into numeric qualities. Each word is coded into a number speaking to its positioning in recurrence. Most incessant words have low numbers; less successive words have higher numbers.

As a starter point, the code imports the IMDb work from Keras and utilizations it to recover the information from the Internet (about a 17.5MB download). The parameters that the model uses envelop only the best 10,000 words and Keras should rearrange the information utilizing a particular arbitrary seed. (Realizing the seed makes it conceivable to replicate the mix as required.) The capacity returns two train and test sets, both made of content successions and the estimation result.

From Keras.datasets import IMDb

top_words = 10000

((x_train, y_train),

(x_test, y_test)) = imdb.load_data(num_words=top_words,

seed=21)

After the past code finishes, you can check the number of models utilizing the accompanying code:

print ("Training examples: %i" % len(x_train))

print ("Test examples: %i" % len(x_test))

In the wake of inquisitive about the quantity of cases accessible for use in the preparation and test period of the neural system, the code yields an answer of 25,000 models for each stage. (This dataset is a moderately little one for a language issue; the dataset is essentially for showing purposes.) what's more, the code decides if the dataset is adjusted, which means it has a practically equivalent number of positive and negative feeling models.

import numpy as np

print (np.unique(y_train, return_counts=True))

The outcome, exhibit ([12500, 12500]), affirms that the dataset is part uniformly among positive and negative results. Such harmony between the reaction classes is only a direct result of the expressive idea of the dataset. In reality, you only occasionally find adjusted datasets. The following stage makes some Python lexicons that can change over

118

between the code utilized in the dataset and the genuine words. The dataset utilized in this model is pre-prepared and gives groupings of numbers speaking to the words, not simply the words. (LSTM and GRU calculations that you find in Keras anticipate successions of numbers as numbers.)

```
word_to_id = {w:i+3 for w,i in imdb.get_word_index().items()}

id_to_word = {0:'<PAD>', 1:'<START>', 2:'<UNK>'}

id_to_word.update({i+3:w for w,i in imdb.get_word_index().items()})

def convert_to_text(sequence):

return ' '.join([id_to_word[s] for s in sequence if s>=3])

print(convert_to_text(x_train))
```

The past code piece characterizes two transformation lexicons (from words to numeric codes and the other way around) and a capacity that makes an interpretation of the dataset models into coherent content. For instance, the code prints the ninth model: "this film resembled an awful train wreck as horrendous as it was ... ". From this extract, you can undoubtedly foresee that the notion for this motion picture isn't sure. Words, for example, terrible, wreck, and ghastly pass on a solid negative inclination, and that makes speculating the right slant simple.

In this model, you get the numeric arrangements and transform them once again into words, yet the inverse is normal. For the most part, you get expressions made up of words and transform them into arrangements of whole numbers to encourage to a layer of RNNs. Keras offers a particular capacity, Tokenizer, which can do that for you. It utilizes the techniques fit_on_text, to figure out how to guide words to whole numbers from preparing information, and texts_to_matrix, to change content into a succession.

Be that as it may, in different expressions, you may not discover such uncovering words for the slant examination. The inclination is communicated in a subtler or aberrant way, and understanding the estimation from the get-go in the content may not be conceivable because noteworthy expressions and words may show up a lot later in the talk. Hence, you likewise need to choose the amount of the expression you need to break down.

Expectedly, you take an underlying piece of the content and utilize it as illustrative of the whole audit. Once in a while, you need a couple of introductory words — for example, the initial 50 words — to get the sense; now and again, you need more. Particularly long messages don't uncover their direction early. It is along these lines up to you to comprehend the kind of content you are working with and choose what number of words to investigate utilizing profound learning. This model considers just the initial 200 words, which should get the job done.

```
from keras.preprocessing.sequence import pad_sequences

max_pad = 200

x_train = pad_sequences(x_train,

maxlen=max_pad)

x_test = pad_sequences(x_test,

maxlen=max_pad)

print(x_train)
```

By utilizing the pad_sequences work from Keras with max_pad set to 200, the code takes the initial 200 expressions of each survey. In the event that the audit contains less than 200 words, the same number of zero qualities as vital go before the arrangement to arrive at the required number of grouping components. Slicing the successions to a specific length and filling the voids with zero qualities is called info cushioning, a significant preparing movement when utilizing RNNs like profound learning calculations. Presently the code plans the engineering:

```
from keras.models import Sequential

from keras.layers import Bidirectional, Dense, Dropout

from keras.layers import GlobalMaxPool1D, LSTM

from keras.layers.embeddings import Embedding
```

```python
embedding_vector_length = 32

model = Sequential()

model.add(Embedding(top_words,

embedding_vector_length,

input_length=max_pad))

model.add(Bidirectional(LSTM(64,
return_sequences=True)))

model.add(GlobalMaxPool1D())

model.add(Dense(16, activation="relu"))

model.add(Dense(1, activation="sigmoid"))

model.compile(loss='binary_crossentropy',

optimizer='adam',

metrics=['accuracy'])

print(model.summary())
```

The past code scrap characterizes the state of the profound learning model, where it utilizes a couple of particular layers for normal language handling from Keras. The model additionally has required an outline of the model (model.summary() order) to figure out what's going on with design by utilizing distinctive neural layers.

You have the Embedding layer, which changes the numeric groupings into a thick word installing. That kind of word installing is progressively reasonable for being scholarly by a layer of RNNs. Keras gives an Embedding layer, which, aside from essentially being the main layer of the system, can achieve two assignments:

Applying pre-trained word installing, (for example, Word2vec or GloVe) to the grouping input. You need to pass the framework containing the installing to its parameter loads.

Making a word inserting without any preparation, in light of the information sources it gets.

In this subsequent case, embedding has to know:

input_dim: The size of the jargon anticipated from information
output_dim: The size of the inserting space that will be delivered (the alleged measurements)
input_length: The grouping size to anticipate

After you decide the parameters, Embedding will locate the better loads to change the groupings into a thick framework during preparing. The thick network size is given by the length of groupings and the dimensionality of the installing.

The model uses Bidirectional wrapping — an LSTM layer of 64 cells. Bidirectional changes an ordinary LSTM layer by multiplying it: On the principal side, it applies the typical arrangement of data sources you give; on the second, it passes the invert of the succession. You utilize this methodology because occasionally, you use words in a different overfitting request, and building a bidirectional layer will get any word design, regardless of the request. The Keras usage is to be sure direct: You apply it as capacity on the layer you need to render bidirectionally.

The bidirectional LSTM is set to return arrangements (return_sequences=True); that is, for every cell, it restores the outcome gave in the wake of seeing every component of the succession. The outcomes, for each succession, are a yield lattice of 200 x 128, where 200 is the number of arrangement components and 128 is the quantity of LSTM cells utilized in the layer. This method keeps the RNN from taking the last aftereffect of each LSTM cell. Clues about the feeling of the content could show up anyplace in the inserted words grouping.

So, it's significant not to take the last aftereffect of every cell, but instead its best consequence. The code in this way depends on the accompanying layer, GlobalMaxPool1D, to check each succession of results given by each LSTM cell and hold just the greatest outcome. That ought to guarantee that the model picks the most grounded sign from each LSTM cell, which is ideally particular by its preparation to pick some significant sign.

After the neural sign is sifted, the model has a layer of 128 yields, one for each LSTM cell. The code diminishes and blends the sign utilizing a progressive thick layer of 16 neurons with ReLU enactment (in this way, making just positive sign go through). The engineering closes with a last hub utilizing sigmoid enactment, which will crush the outcomes into the 0–1 territory and make them look like probabilities.

Having characterized the engineering, you would now be able to prepare the system to perform a conclusion investigation. Three ages (passing the information multiple times through the system to have it become familiar with the examples) will do the trick. The code uses groups of 256 audits each time, which enables the system to see enough assortment of words and estimations each time before refreshing its loads utilizing backpropagation. At long last, the code centers around the outcomes given by the approval information (which isn't a piece of the preparation information). Getting a decent outcome from the approval information implies the neural net is preparing the info effectively. The code provides details regarding approval information soon after every age wraps up.

```
history = model.fit(x_train, y_train,

validation_data=(x_test, y_test),

epochs=3, batch_size=256)
```

Getting the outcomes takes some time, yet if you are utilizing a GPU, it will finish in the time you take to drink some espresso. Now, you can assess the outcomes, again utilizing the approval information. (The outcomes shouldn't have any shocks or contrasts from what the code detailed during preparing.)

loss, metric = model.evaluate(x_test, y_test, verbose=0)

print ("Test accuracy: %0.3f" % metric)

The last precision, which is the level of right answers from the profound neural system, will be an estimation of around 85—86 percent. The outcome will change somewhat each time you run the trial as a result of randomization when building your neural system. That is consummately ordinary, given the little size of the information you are working with. If you start with the privilege fortunate loads, the learning will be simpler in such a short instructional meeting.

At last, your system is an opinion analyzer that can figure the notion communicated in a motion picture audit effectively around 85 percent of the time. Given considerably all the more preparing information and increasingly advanced neural models, you can get results that are much progressively noteworthy. In advertising, a comparable instrument is utilized to robotize numerous procedures that require perusing content and making a move. Once more, you could couple a system like this with a neural system that tunes in to a voice and transforms it into the content. (This is another use of RNNs, presently fueling Alexa, Siri,

Google Voice, and numerous other individual partners.) The progress enables the application to comprehend the supposition even in vocal articulations, for example, a telephone call from a client.

THE BASICS OF DECISION TREES

The point with any decision tree is to make a serviceable model that will anticipate the estimation of an objective variable dependent on the arrangement of information factors. This segment clarifies where choice trees are utilized alongside a portion of the favorable circumstances and restrictions of choice trees. In this area, you additionally discover how a choice tree is determined physically so you can see the math in question.

Utilizations for Decision Trees

Consider how you select various choices inside a computerized phone call. The choices are choices that are being made for you to get to the ideal office. These choice trees are utilized successfully in numerous industry regions.

In alternative valuing, a double like the choice tree is utilized to foresee the cost of a choice in either a bull or bear showcase.

Advertisers use choice trees to set up clients by sort and anticipate whether a client will purchase a particular kind of item.

In the medicinal field, choice tree models have been intended to analyze blood contaminations or even anticipate cardiovascular failure results in chest torment patients. Factors in the choice tree incorporate analysis, treatment, and patient information.

The gaming business currently utilizes numerous choice trees in development acknowledgment and facial acknowledgment. The Microsoft Kinect stage utilizes this strategy to track body development. The Kinect group utilized one million pictures and prepared three trees. Inside one day, and utilizing a 1,000-center bunch, the choice trees were arranging explicit body parts over the screen.

Focal points of Decision Trees

There are some valid justifications to utilize choice trees. For a certain something, they are anything but difficult to peruse. After a model is produced, it's anything but difficult to report back to others concerning how the tree functions. Additionally, with choice trees, you can deal with numerical or ordered data. Afterward, this part shows how to function through an algorithm with classification esteems physically; the model walkthrough utilizes numerical information.

As far as information arrangement, there's little to do. For whatever length of time that the information is formalized in something like comma isolated factors, at that point, you can make a working model. This likewise makes it simple to approve the model utilizing different

128

tests. With choice trees, you utilize white-box testing—which means the inner operations can be watched however not transformed; you can see the means that are being utilized when the tree is being displayed. Choice trees perform well with sensible measures of processing power. If you have an enormous arrangement of information, at that point, choice tree learning will deal with it well.

Constraints of Decision Trees

With each arrangement of favorable circumstances, there's normally a lot of disservices sitting out of sight. One of the primary issues of choice trees is that they can make excessively complex models, contingent upon the information introduced in the preparation set.

To keep away from the ML algorithm's over-fitting the information, it's occasionally worth exploring the preparation information and pruning the qualities to classifications, which will create a more refined and better-tuned model. A portion of the choice tree ideas can be difficult to learn because the model can't express them effectively. This inadequacy once in a while brings about a bigger than-ordinary model. You may be required to change the model or take a gander at various techniques for ML.

Trees made with C4.5 are pruned after creation; the calculation will return to the hubs and choose if a hub is adding to the outcome in the tree. If it isn't, at that point, it's supplanted with a leaf hub.

CHAID

The CHAID (Chi-squared Automatic Interaction Detection) strategy was created by Gordon V. Kass in 1980. The principle utilization of it was inside advertising, yet it was additionally utilized inside therapeutic and mental research.

MARS

For numerical information, it may merit exploring the MARS (multivariate versatile relapse splines) calculation. You may consider this to be an open-source option called "Earth," as MARS is trademarked by Salford Systems.

Throughout the years, there have been different calculations created for choice tree investigation. A portion of the more typical ones is recorded here.

ID3

The ID3 (Iterative Dichotomiser 3) algorithm was imagined by Ross Quinlan to make trees from datasets. By computing the entropy for each characteristic in the dataset, this could be part of subsets dependent on the base entropy esteem. After the set had a choice tree hub made, every one of that was required was to experience the rest of the traits in the set recursively.

ID3 utilizes the technique for data gain—the proportion of distinction in entropy when a character is a part—to settle on the root hub (the hub with the most noteworthy data gain).

ID3 experienced over-fitting on preparing data, and the algorithm was more qualified to littler trees than enormous ones. The ID3 calculation is utilized less nowadays for the C4.5 algorithms, which is plot straightaway.

C4.5

Quinlan returned for a reprise with the C4.5 algorithms. It's likewise founded on the data gain technique; however, it empowers the trees to be utilized for classification. This is a broadly utilized calculation in that numerous clients keep running in Weka with the open-source Java adaptation of C4.5, the J48 algorithm. There are striking enhancements in C4.5 over the first ID3 calculation. With the capacity to chip away at consistent traits, the C4.5 techniques will figure a limit point for the split to happen. For instance, with a rundown of qualities like the accompanying:

85,80,83,70,68,65,64,72,69,75,75,72,81,71

C4.5 will work out a split point for the trait (an) and give a straightforward choice rule of:

a <= 80 or a > 80

C4.5 can work regardless of missing characteristic qualities. The missing qualities are set apart with a question mark (?). The addition and entropy counts are just skipped when there is no information accessible.

Building a Decision Tree

Decision trees are worked around the essential idea of this algorithm.

- Check the model for the base cases.

- Iterate through every one of the traits (attr).

- Get the standardized data gain from parting on attr.

- Let best_attr be the property with the most noteworthy data gain.

- Create a choice hub that parts on the best_attr characteristic.

- Work on the sublists that are gotten by parting on best_attr and include those hubs as youngster hubs.

That is the essential diagram of what happens when you assemble a choice tree

CHAPTER SEVEN
CHALLENGES OF MACHINE LEARNING

ML and AI aren't something out of science fiction motion pictures any longer; it's particularly a reality. While we took numerous decades to arrive, late overwhelming speculation inside this space has fundamentally quickened improvement.

While ML is making critical walks inside digital security and independent autos, this portion overall still has far to go. This is because ML hasn't had the option to defeat various difficulties that still disrupt the general flow of advancement.

What are these difficulties?

1. Memory systems

Memory systems or memory expanded neural systems still require huge working memory to store information. This sort of neural system should be snared to a memory obstruct that can be both composed and perused by the system.

This is a noteworthy obstacle that ML needs to survive. To achieve genuinely productive and powerful AI, we need to locate a superior strategy for systems to find realities, store them, and consistently get to them when required.

2. Natural language handling (NLP)

Albeit a great deal of cash and time has been contributed, despite everything, we have far to go to accomplish normal language preparing and comprehension of language.

This is as yet an enormous test notwithstanding for deep networks. Right now, we instruct PCs to speak to dialects and reenact thinking dependent on that. Be that as it may, this has been reliably poor.

3. Consideration

Human visual frameworks use consideration in an exceptionally hearty way to incorporate a rich arrangement of highlights. In any case, right now, ML is tied in with concentrating on little lumps of information boosts, each in turn, and afterward, incorporate the outcomes toward the end.

For ML to genuinely understand its potential, we need instruments that work as a human visual framework to be incorporated with neural systems. At present, we're utilizing a softmax capacity to get to memory squares, however as a general rule, consideration is intended to be non-differentiable.

4. See deep nets training

Even though ML has made significant progress, regardless, we don't realize precisely how profound nets preparing work. So if we don't have the foggiest idea of how preparing nets really work, how would we gain any genuine ground?

5. One-shot learning

While uses of neural systems have advanced, despite everything, we haven't had the option to accomplish one-shot learning. Up until this point, customary inclination based systems need a gigantic measure of information to learn, and this is regularly as broad iterative preparing.

Rather, we need to figure out how to empower neural systems to pick up utilizing only a couple of models.

6. Deep reinforcement learning to control robots

If we can make sense of how to empower profound support figuring out how to control robots, we can make characters like C-3PO a reality (well, kind of). Indeed, when you permit profound fortification learning, you empower ML to handle more difficult issues. Existing fortification learning calculations additionally work at a solitary time scale, and this makes it hard for these techniques to learn in issues that include altogether different time scales. For instance, the support learning calculation that figures out how to drive a vehicle by keeping it inside the traffic path can't likewise figure out how to plan courses starting with one area then onto the next, because these choices happen at altogether different time scales. Research in various leveled fortification learning is endeavoring to address this issue.

7. Verification, Validation, and Trust.

Customary programming frameworks regularly contain bugs, but since programming architects can peruse the program code, they can plan great tests to watch that the product is working effectively. Yet, the consequence of AI is a 'discovery' framework that acknowledges information sources and creates yields yet is hard to investigate. Henceforth, an exceptionally dynamic subject in AI research is to create techniques for making AI frameworks increasingly interpretable (for example, by giving clarifications or making an interpretation of their outcomes into straightforward structures). There is likewise explore on mechanized strategies for confirmation and approval of discovery frameworks. One of the most intriguing new headings is to make mechanized 'enemies' that endeavor to break the AI framework. These can frequently find inputs that reason the educated program to come up short.

A related territory of research is 'robust machine learning.' We look for ML algorithms that function admirably, notwithstanding when their suppositions are damaged. The greatest presumption in AI is that the preparation information is thought to be autonomously appropriated and to be a delegate case of things to come contribution to the framework. A few scientists are investigating methods for making ML frameworks increasingly powerful to disappointments of this supposition.

8. Video preparing information

We presently can't seem to use video preparing information; rather, we as yet depend on static pictures. To enable ML frameworks to work better, we have to empower them to learn by tuning in and watching. Video datasets will, in general, be a lot more extravagant than static pictures. Thus, we people have been exploiting learning by watching our dynamic world. Is there any valid reason why machines shouldn't be empowered to do likewise?

ORGANIZING THE MACHINE LEARNING PROCESS AND CHALLENGES

In the midst of testing, fiddling, and a great deal of inward R&D-type exercises, we attempted to pull a few strings of coherence through the procedures our group was iteratively ordering in the quest for information science. We truly investigated our ML, Deep Learning, and Unsupervised Learning methods, just as our progressively customary factual methodologies, and built up a cycle that incorporates all the important advances while taking into consideration adjustment for non-conventional or particular uses of information science. The procedure is separated into the four-quadrant lifecycle of ML.

The four quadrants are:

- Project Design
- Data Preparation
- Model Fitting
- Inference and Deployment

Quadrant One: Project Design

As anyone might expect, the principal quadrant centers around choosing the suitable techniques to address the prescient, expository, or mechanization job needing to be done. It is one of the most troublesome stages in the lifecycle and one that requires much-coordinated effort among researchers and leaders.

Since AI and ML have moved toward becoming popular expressions in the specialized network, the greatest test in quadrant one comes down to deciding if the issue genuinely requires an ML arrangement. It is conceivable a progressed expository, measurable, or another methodology could get the job done. Standard speaking, the ideal approach to decide if an ML arrangement is required is to solicit chiefs to finish one from the two after sentences:

"We have to computerize X because... "
"We have to foresee X because... "

The way to deal with this stage contains four stages:
Wanted Output Determination
Target Data Identification
Model Selection
Philosophy Engineering

While ontology building is seemingly the most included advance in the principal quadrant, the greatest difficulties happen during the time spent recognizing the objective information accessible and deciding the model most appropriate for the errand. When we've done those two things, it is on to the undertaking on which the main part within recent memory is spent: information wrangling.

Quadrant Two: Data Preparation

A test well-known to all associated with data science is pre-handling and naming information. The procedure of information wrangling (i.e., moving information to a focal storehouse and changing it into a composition helpful for ingest into a famous ML system) winds up requiring significantly more time than the genuine model tuning and testing itself. Nonetheless, information marking is the biggest test as there is, by all accounts, nothing more than trouble approach to dodge intolerable human capital costs and long periods of monotonous, mistake inclined work. The particular strides inside this stage are:

- Data Wrangling and Cleaning
- Highlight Engineering
- Data Labeling

The phase that pursues information arrangement is regularly the stage individuals most promptly partner with the field of information science. The third stage includes genuine information researchers (rather than information specialists and programming designers) as thorough testing and assessment must be coordinated towards model tuning and execution.

Quadrant Three: Model Fitting

Although the greater part of the work occurs during the information readiness and naming stage (quadrant two), model planning is the fundamentals of ML. This stage incorporates three stages:

+ Cloud Architecting
+ Model Training
+ Model Evaluation and Validation

The most conspicuous test in this stage is in the exactness arithmetic (and a ton of experimentation) that leads to display approval through hyperparameter tuning and model testing.

Quadrant Four: Inference and Deployment

Now in our ML Lifecycle, the group is set up to use the model to make reasonable forecasts, post-process the outcomes, and imagine them. This is a joint exertion that includes examiners, information researchers, and UI/UX engineers. At times, contingent upon the errand, specific representation strategies are required, for example, present procedure triangulation calculations on ascertaining an increasingly exact area for an anticipated article. The three stages are:

+ Forecast
+ Post-preparing and Visualization
+ Operational Deployment

Expecting the model is producing precise outcomes that are outwardly spoken to, all that is left is for it to be utilized for its proposed reason. In the National Security condition, operational organization of AI calculations is perhaps the greatest test, both due to register control imperatives of downrange situations and disparities between unclassified preparing information and the mission information on which the model might be relied upon to perform derivation.

THE THREAT OF ADVANCED AI

Like every single innovation, AI is unquestionably going to change the activity showcase. Employments that include straightforward monotonous movement—regardless of whether it is repeated physical activities (like plant work and truck driving) or repeated scholarly activities (like much work in law, bookkeeping, and medication)— will probably be in any event somewhat supplanted by programming and robots. Similarly, as with the Industrial Revolution, there is probably going to be a huge disturbance in the economy as these new advances are created. The significant inquiry is whether ML and AI will likewise make new sorts of occupations. This additionally happened during the Industrial Revolution, and it could happen again in the AI upset. It is difficult to anticipate what these occupations will be.

One part of numerous human employments that I accept will be hard to robotize is compassion. Robots and AI frameworks will have different encounters than humans altogether. In contrast to

144

individuals, they won't have the option to 'set up themselves into an individual's perspective to comprehend and sympathize with people. Rather, they should be instructed, similar to outsiders or like Commander Data in Star Trek, to anticipate and comprehend human feelings. Interestingly, individuals are normally ready to do these things, since we as a whole know 'what it feels like' to be human. So occupations that include sympathy (for example directing, training, the board, client assistance) are most drastically averse to be acceptably mechanized. This will be especially valid if human clients place an incentive on 'real human association' instead of tolerating a cooperation with a robot or mechanized framework.

On the off chance that most mechanical and horticultural generation ends up computerized—and if the subsequent riches are uniformly conveyed all through society—at that point, people are probably going to discover different activities with their time. Venturing out to visit different nations and different societies will probably turn out to be significantly more prominent than it is today. Sports, games, music, and expressions of the human experience may likewise turn out to be considerably more well known. One hundred years prior, it was difficult to get a back rub or a pedicure. Presently these are accessible all over. Who realizes what individuals will need to do and what encounters they will need to have a long time from now?

There are two diverse prevalent thoughts of the 'peculiarity.' One thought, exemplified by the compositions of Ray Kurzweil, is that due to the exponential improvement of numerous advances, it is hard for us to see exceptionally far into what's to come. This is the possibility of an 'innovative peculiarity.' A genuine numerical peculiarity would be the time when innovation improves boundlessly rapidly. However, this is unimaginable, because there are cutoff points to all advances (even though we don't have the foggiest idea of what they are). There is a celebrated law in financial matters because of Herbert Stein: 'If something can't go on always, it won't.' This is valid for Moore's Law, and it is valid for all AI advancements. Be that as it may, regardless of whether a genuine numerical peculiarity is outlandish, we are as of now encountering exponential development in the capacities of AI frameworks, so their future abilities will be altogether different from their present capacities, and standard extrapolation is incomprehensible. So I trust Kurzweil is right that we can't see extremely far into this exponentially-evolving future.

There is a second idea of 'peculiarity' that alludes to the ascent of supposed genius. The contention—first set forth by I.J. Great in an article in 1965—is that sooner or later, AI innovation will cross an edge where it will have the option to improve itself recursively, and afterward, it will quickly improve and turn out to be exponentially more intelligent than individuals. It will be the 'last creation' of humankind. Regularly, the edge is thought to be 'human-level AI,' where the AI framework matches human knowledge. I am not persuaded by this contention for a few reasons.

To start with, the entire objective of AI is to make PC frameworks that can adapt independently. This is a type of personal growth (and regularly it is applied to improve the learning framework itself and thus is recursive personal development). Be that as it may, such frameworks have always been unable to improve themselves past one emphasis. That is, they improve themselves, yet then the subsequent framework can't improve itself. The purpose behind this is we detail the issue as an issue of capacity streamlining, and once you have discovered the ideal estimation of that work, further advancement can't improve it, by definition.

To keep up exponential enhancements, each innovation requires rehashed leaps forward. Moore's Law, for instance, is not a solitary procedure, yet a staircase of upgrades where each 'progression' included an alternate leap forward. This leads us back to the Kurzweil-type innovative peculiarity as opposed to genius.

Second, it is exceptionally suspicious that the contentions about genius set the edge to coordinate human insight. This strikes me as a similar mistake that was uncovered by Copernicus and by Darwin. People are probably not unique at all as for the knowledge that PCs can achieve. The breaking points we experience are presumably managed by numerous components, including the size and processing intensity of our cerebrums, the terms of our lives, and the way that every last one of us must learn alone (as opposed to like parallel and disseminated PCs). PCs are as of now more astute than individuals on a wide scope

147

of assignments including employment shop booking, course arranging, control of a flying machine, the recreation of complex frameworks (for example the air), web search, memory, number juggling, certain types of hypothesis demonstrating, etc. Be that as it may, none of these super-human capacities has driven the sort of genius portrayed by Good.

Third, we see in people that insight will, in general, include broadness instead of profundity. An incredible physicist, for example, Stephen Hawking, is a lot more intelligent than me about cosmology, yet I am more proficient than he is about AI. Moreover, tests have uncovered that individuals who are specialists in a single part of the human undertaking are no superior to average in most different viewpoints. This recommends the analogy of insight as rungs on a stepping stool, which is simply the premise of the contention on recursive personal development, is an inappropriate allegory. Instead, we ought to consider the allegory of a fluid spreading over the outside of a table or the analogy of biodiversity where each part of information fills a specialty in the downpour timberland of human insight. This representation doesn't propose that there is some limit that, once surpassed, will prompt genius.

At last, the case that Kurzweil's perspective on the peculiarity is the correct one doesn't imply that AI innovation is innately protected and that we don't have anything to stress over. A long way from it. In reality, as PCs become progressively keen, we are propelled to place them accountable for high-hazard basic leadership, for example, controlling self-driving autos, dealing with the power lattice, or battling wars (as self-sufficient weapon frameworks).

CONCLUSION

The fields of machining adapting, profound learning, and computerized reasoning are quickly extending and are probably going to keep on doing as such for a long time to come. There are many main impetuses for this, as quickly caught in this review. Now and again, the advancement has been emotional, opening new ways to deal with long-standing innovation challenges, for example, progresses in PC vision and picture investigation. Those capacities alone are opening new pathways and applications in the ICME/MGI area. In different examples, the instruments have just given transformative advancement up until this point, for example, in many parts of computational mechanics and mechanical conduct of materials. As a rule, the fields of materials and procedures science and building, just as basic mechanics and configuration, are slacking other specialized teaches in grasping ML/DL/AI devices and investigating how they may profit by them. Nor are these fields utilizing their imposing establishments in material science and profound comprehension of their information to add to the ML/DL/AI fields. Regardless, innovation pioneers and those related with MPSE ought to expect unforeseeable and progressive effects crosswise over almost the whole area of materials and structures, procedures, and multiscale displaying and reproduction throughout the following two decades. In this regard, what's to come is presently, and it is suitable to make prompt interests in carrying these devices into the MPSE fields and their instructive procedures.